MONADNOCK
MOMENTS

Monadnock Moments

Historic Tales *from* Southwest New Hampshire

Alan F. Rumrill

The History Press

Published by The History Press
Charleston, SC 29403
www.historypress.net

Front and back cover: Oil paintings of Mount Monadnock by William Preston Phelps.
Courtesy of Marie Royce Ruffle.

All photos courtesy of the Historical Society of Cheshire County.

First published 2009

Manufactured in the United States

ISBN 978.1.59629.740.1

Library of Congress Cataloging-in-Publication Data

Rumrill, Alan F.
Monadnock moments : historic tales from southwest New Hampshire / Alan F. Rumrill.
p. cm.
ISBN 978-1-59629-740-1
1. Monadnock, Mount, Region (N.H.)--History--Anecdotes. 2. Monadnock, Mount, Region (N.H.)--Description and travel. I. Title.
F42.C5R86 2009
974.2'9--dc22
2009036542

Notice: The information in this book is true and complete to the best of our knowledge. It is offered without guarantee on the part of the author or The History Press. The author and The History Press disclaim all liability in connection with the use of this book.

Contents

Acknowledgements

I must begin by expressing my appreciation to the board of trustees of the Historical Society of Cheshire County for its support of this project and of the *Monadnock Moments* radio program. This book would not have been possible without its enthusiastic support of the development and airing of the *Moments* program for twenty years.

I also want to thank Marie Royce Ruffle for sharing the wonderful Mount Monadnock painting by William Preston Phelps that graces the cover of this book. Acknowledgement also goes to Julie Dickson, who spent hours arranging and formatting the text; Kathy Schillemat also assisted with the preparation of the text for publication. The editorial skills of Catherine Behrens were essential in converting the *Moments* from radio script to book text.

Finally, it would be impossible to share these historical vignettes without the work of the many individuals in the past who recorded the information on which these stories are based. This includes local historians who consciously wrote history, but it also includes town clerks, court scribes, newspaper reporters and many others who recorded details every day that have now become history. Their work makes it possible for us to share history for the enlightenment of current and future generations.

Introduction

Twenty-five years ago I was given a cassette tape containing a number of short local historical tales that had been prepared for a Peterborough, New Hampshire radio station by Fritz Wetherbee. The idea of local history vignettes delivered via the airwaves appealed to me. This might be a new way for the Historical Society of Cheshire County to share Monadnock regional history and to gain more exposure at the same time. I approached a Keene radio station, which agreed to give the society radio time if I would research, write and deliver the programs.

Since that time, Fritz Wetherbee has moved from radio to television and has perfected the art of telling stories of New Hampshire history via that medium. My first radio program, named *Monadnock Moments*, was played on radio station WKNE AM in July 1985. For the next twenty years, I researched and recorded a new *Moment* to be played each week—more than one thousand recordings in all. These two-minute historical tales were presented as a public service by WKNE and the historical society.

The radio was a way for us to share history with a much wider audience than we normally reached—an audience that might not visit the historical society to learn about local history through the organization's other programs. *Monadnock Moments* also helped me to learn more about local history and to present it in a way that was entertaining to others. I immersed myself in research once a month to find tales that were a little out of the ordinary. Successful businessmen, politicians and soldiers were included in the *Moments*, but so were tales of disaster, murder, wild animals, con men and the resourcefulness and accomplishments of the ordinary residents of southwest New Hampshire. The most popular stories were those that illustrated how individuals lived, worked and persevered in the past. Listeners could take something from those stories and use them as guides in the present.

Many *Monadnock Moments* listeners encouraged the historical society to publish the *Moments* over the years, but that was not seriously considered until The History Press approached the society and asked us to do exactly that. This book contains more than one hundred *Moments* that have never been compiled in print before. Some of these tales are familiar to local history buffs, but some had never been shared publicly before they were aired on the radio. We hope that all of them will entertain readers and help them to understand more clearly how the Monadnock region developed into the unique place that it is today.

Colonial History

Dr. Obadiah Blake

Dr. Obadiah Blake, born in Wrentham, Massachusetts, in 1719, was one of the first settlers of Keene in the late 1730s. He was also one of the first physicians in the town, serving the region for many years.

Dr. Blake's account book from the late eighteenth century gives us a view of a medical profession quite different from what we are familiar with today. Most of his work involved house calls. He traveled far and wide, with regular customers in Croydon, New Hampshire; Athens, Vermont; and Royalston, Massachusetts. He traveled on horseback, with his medicines and instruments in his saddlebags.

Dr. Blake's fees were small and usually paid in vegetables, grain or other produce. Joshua Osgood paid two bushels of beans for several visits and medicines in 1785. Asahel Blake paid his one pound, two shilling bill with "one house clock" in 1786. Francis Drake paid his medical bill by chopping wood for Dr. Blake. It was common for Dr. Blake not to be paid at all. For example, one account was settled "by running away," and another was "cancelled in full by poverty." The one pound, ten shilling account of Robert McNeal was "settled by death."

Despite the long hours, small or nonexistent pay and long journeys in all types of weather, Dr. Blake lived a long and full life. He passed away in 1810 at the age of ninety-two. Dr. Blake bequeathed his saddlebags, vials and lancet to his son Obadiah Jr., who had followed his father into the field of medicine.

Warning Out of Town

One of the more unfriendly customs practiced by our ancestors was known as "warning out of town." When a new family that did not own land arrived in town during the 1770s, 1780s and 1790s, the constable would often pay them a visit and warn them to leave town.

This custom was not as cruel as it seems. Laws were in place that required that poor people should be cared for at the expense of the town where they settled. If a new family arrived that the selectmen thought might become a welfare burden, they would send the constable with a warrant to warn the family out of town. In reality, this was a legal maneuver, and the people were not truly expected to leave the town. If a warrant of this type was recorded within one year of the date when a family arrived, the town could not be held responsible for their care in the future.

Most local towns used this procedure; the record of warnings out of Keene is still on file at the city clerk's office. Original warning out records survive for Surry. In October 1794, the selectmen of that town ordered more than twenty people to depart the town of Surry and return to the towns from whence they came. The selectmen of Dublin warned more than one hundred families out of town between 1777 and 1788.

This unkind practice of warning people out of town was generally discontinued by 1800. Many of the people who were warned out because they might become a burden eventually went on to become wealthy citizens and taxpayers. Nathan Bixby in Dublin, for example, was warned out of town in 1778. Three years later, he was elected selectman and for many years was the highest taxpayer in town.

Blake Among the Indians

Nathan Blake came from Wrentham, Massachusetts, as one of the first settlers of Keene in 1736. He built a home here and began a family with his wife, Elizabeth.

Several years later, during 1745, war was declared between France and England. The Indians to the north became allies of the French, and Keene residents were soon in danger of attack. On April 23, 1746, the fort at Keene was indeed attacked by a war party of about one hundred Indians. Nathan Blake

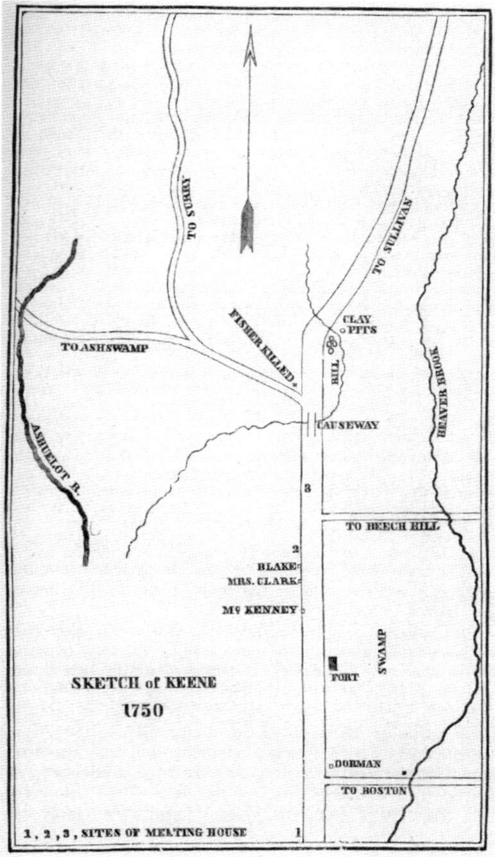

Map of Keene in 1750 showing Nathan Blake's house and the fort.

was at his homestead when the alarm was sounded. In an attempt to save his cattle, he took a few moments to open his barn door. By the time he finished this chore, his escape route was cut off, and the Indians captured him. Blake was bound and led away as a captive.

He was taken to Montreal, where his captors forced him to run the gauntlet. His strength so impressed the Indians that he was able to gain their respect. Shortly thereafter, he was sent as a military prisoner to an Indian village just north of Quebec. Once again he gained acceptance and great respect throughout his new community. Consequently, upon the death of one of the local chiefs, Blake was given the chief's authority and privileges, as well as his wife.

Despite his rank among the Indians, Blake longed for Keene. He made a deal with the Indians whereby they agreed to release him if he would build them a house such as the English had. Blake's Indian wife opposed the deal, but he refused to stay in the village. The house was built, Blake turned himself over to French authorities in Quebec and he was given his freedom in an exchange of prisoners of war in April 1748, two years after he had been taken prisoner.

Blake returned to his wife Elizabeth and to his children. They all returned to Keene in 1749. He lived in Keene for sixty-two more years until his death at age ninety-nine.

NATHAN BLAKE'S AGREEMENT

Today we often hear about prenuptial agreements involving movie stars whose spouses agree to receive a specific amount of money as a settlement if the marriage should fail. Marriage agreements are really nothing new; in fact, one of Keene's very first settlers, Nathan Blake, entered into such an agreement more than two hundred years ago.

Blake was one of Keene's most prominent and respected citizens for nearly seventy-five years during Keene's early days. He married Elizabeth Graves in 1742. Nathan and Elizabeth spent sixty-two years together until her death in 1804.

Two years later, at the age of ninety-four, Nathan decided to remarry and entered into a marriage agreement with Mrs. Mary Brintnall. The agreement stated that the two would be married and that Mary Brintnall would live with Blake and take care of him in sickness and health until his death. At that time she would be entitled to $100 from Blake's estate. When she had received her $100, Mary agreed to return to her former home and to make no further claim against the estate. Furthermore, she agreed to "procure and find her own clothes in addition to taking care of Blake during his lifetime."

The agreement was signed by Nathan, Mary and two witnesses on December 30, 1805. Three days later, Nathan and Mary became husband and wife. It is recorded that Mary Brintnall was "a fascinating widow of sixty-four" at the time of the wedding. Mary and Nathan spent five years together until Nathan passed away in 1811 at the age of ninety-nine. Shortly thereafter, his estate awarded "widow Mary Blake as per agreement before marriage…$100." Widow Mary Brintnall Blake passed away in Keene fourteen years later at the age of eighty-five.

SLAVERY IN CHESHIRE COUNTY

When we think of slavery in the United States, we often think of the plantations of the Deep South and of the Civil War that divided the Union. Most people are surprised to learn that Cheshire County was the home of eighteen slaves at the time of the first census in 1790.

Eleven of the county's eighteen slaves resided with families in Hinsdale, Keene, Stoddard, Walpole, Westmoreland and Winchester; the remaining seven lived in towns that are now part of Sullivan County. Slave labor did not fit well into New Hampshire's economy of subsistence farming. Most slaves acted as servants in the homes of well-to-do families.

Although the names of the county's slave owners of 1790 have been preserved, most of these people have been otherwise forgotten. General James Reed is probably the best remembered of the group. He was one of the first settlers of Fitzwilliam and did much to aid the growth of that town. He attained the rank of brigadier general during the Revolutionary War while serving under General Washington. By 1790, when he was recorded as owning a slave, he was blind and quite elderly.

The social and economic conditions in Cheshire County did not support the development of slavery, and it did not last long in the county or the state. There were 158 slaves in all of New Hampshire in 1790, only 8 by 1800 and the population census of 1820 did not list any.

Bathsheba Day's Ride

Ebenezer Day was one of the first settlers of Keene in the 1730s. He settled in the north part of the town, on what is now the East Surry Road near the Surry town line. This location, which was good for farming, was far from the fort on Keene's Main Street and thus exposed to Indian attack.

Day farmed, operated a gristmill and had opened a tavern by 1754. There was still fear of Indian raids as late as 1755, and Ebenezer Day and his wife Bathsheba must have watched the forest carefully as they worked on the farm and cared for their young children. They had two daughters by that time, Ruth, age four, and one-year-old Bathsheba. One day a warning came to hurry to the fort because a group of Indians had killed a woman in the village.

Ebenezer and Bathsheba gathered up young Ruth, placed Bathsheba in a meal sack, climbed on the horse and rode as fast as possible toward the fort four miles away. Mrs. Day clung to her husband with one hand and used the other to hold the meal sack, which bounced off the side of the moving horse. The family reached the fort safely. When they climbed down from the horse and opened the sack, however, they found that the baby was upside down and had made the four-mile journey on her head.

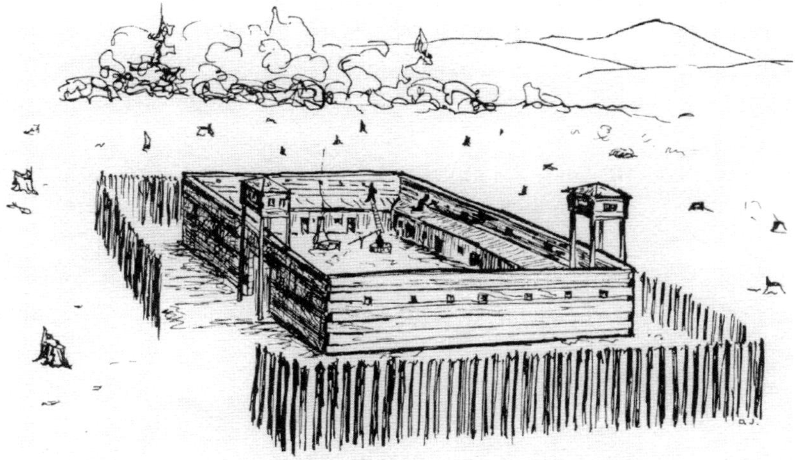

The fort on Keene's Main Street.

Amazingly, Bathsheba had suffered no ill effects from her perilous ride. Twenty-five years later, she married Nathan Blake Jr. Nathan's father, Nathan Sr., had himself been captured by Indians and held captive in Canada for two years. Nathan Jr. and Bathsheba, children of the French and Indian Wars, eventually raised eight children of their own in Keene.

ABIGAIL HALE

Nathan Hale was a prominent resident of Rindge, New Hampshire, during the 1760s and 1770s. He was a storekeeper, farmer and the owner of large tracts of land. Early in 1766, Hale married Abigail Grout, the daughter of the first settler in Jaffrey. Abigail was a strong-willed, outspoken woman who, unlike most of the women of her day, has not been forgotten by succeeding generations.

Nathan Hale served in the Revolutionary War. He had risen to the rank of colonel when he was captured by the British and died as a prisoner of war on Long Island in September 1780. This left Abigail as a thirty-five-year-old widow with six children ranging in age from ten months to thirteen years. Nathan left a large estate, which Abigail managed on her own.

Although he was a prominent merchant and farmer, Nathan's large acreage made the property taxes a great burden to Abigail. Taxes were high at the time to support the war effort. She petitioned the New Hampshire legislature for relief from taxation because her husband had served in the Continental army for five years and she had a large and helpless family to support. She based her argument against paying taxes on a principle well known to the Americans of her day. Abigail claimed that one reason we were fighting the Revolution was to overcome the tyranny of taxation without representation. With her husband gone, she was paying the taxes on the family property, but as a woman she was not allowed to vote. She felt that she was being taxed without being able to represent herself in the government. She refused to pay her taxes and, as a result, was arrested and spent a month in jail. Abigail Hale is remembered by the people of Rindge as one of the first women's suffrage advocates in America.

The Keene Raid

No Revolutionary War battles were fought in Cheshire County, and few armed confrontations took place here during the Revolutionary period. One such confrontation, now known as the Keene Raid, did occur here in May 1779. It illustrates the revolutionary spirit that was present in the region.

In Keene at that time, there were several families who were loyal to the government of Great Britain. Some of the local Patriots felt that these Loyalists were secretly storing supplies for the British army. Several zealous Patriots convinced Captain Elisha Mack of Gilsum to lead a band of men into Keene to punish the Loyalists. Mack and his company arrived in Keene at sunrise on the morning of May 31, 1779. They seized the Loyalists and confined them to a room at Hall's Tavern. The mob then searched the homes for contraband provisions but found none.

By this time, the Keene militia had been alerted and arrived on the scene. Colonel Alexander, leading the militia, assembled his men on the common, facing Captain Mack, who had his men drawn up several hundred feet down Main Street. Colonel Alexander approached Mack and demanded to know if he planned to continue his illegal raid. "I do," Mack replied, "at the hazard of my life." Colonel Alexander responded, "Then you must prepare for eternity, for you shall not be permitted to take vengeance in this irregular mode on any men, even if they are Tories." This speech, backed by the armed militia, cooled the spirit of the mob. They released their prisoners and marched silently toward Gilsum. The women of Keene accompanied the marchers, beating on pans and kettles until the mob was out of view. A long poem about the event was soon written and distributed throughout the area, thereby immortalizing the Keene Raid of 1779.

Dorcas Perry's Tragedy

The Perrys were a typical family of colonial New Hampshire. Ebenezer and Dorcas Perry came to the wilderness of Nelson, New Hampshire, shortly before the Revolutionary War. They were accompanied by their six young children and one older boy, Ichabod, who had been born to Ebenezer's first wife.

When the Revolutionary War began, Ebenezer went to serve the Patriot cause and left Dorcas at home to care for the children. Ebenezer served at Portsmouth, New York, Ticonderoga and Bennington. In March 1777, Ichabod also enlisted in the army at age fifteen. During the summer of that year, the six youngsters became ill with dysentery. Late in August, as Dorcas tended the children, she received word that Ebenezer had been killed in a skirmish with Tories and Indians at the Battle of Bennington. Soon thereafter, all six of the children, Hannah, John, Jacob, Dorcas, Jonathan and young Ebenezer, aged ten months to eleven years, died of the disease, leaving their mother alone.

A few months later, the Perry home burned to the ground, leaving her homeless as well. Dorcas sold the land to a neighbor for a small amount and left town brokenhearted. A few old roses that bloom each June alongside the empty cellar hole are the only hints left today of Dorcas Perry's time in Nelson.

The Ninth State

A grand celebration was held in Keene, New Hampshire, on June 30, 1788. A parade of horsemen traveled to Swanzey in the morning and returned to Keene at two o'clock in the afternoon. Upon their return, they were joined by other local citizens and were accompanied by music as they paraded through the town.

The group proceeded to a small hill in the village where the Reverend Aaron Hall presented an eloquent speech. After the speech, thirteen toasts were drunk. Following each toast, guns were fired and the crowd cheered. At eight o'clock in the evening a forty-foot bonfire was ignited and fireworks were exhibited. The day ended with an elegant ball.

Why were Keene's 1,300 residents indulging in such a grand celebration? Nine days earlier, the state of New Hampshire had voted, by the narrow margin of fifty-seven to forty-seven, to adopt the Constitution of the United States. Although Cheshire County had voted eleven to ten against ratification, Keene's representative, the Reverend Aaron Hall, had voted in favor. New Hampshire was the ninth and deciding state to vote favorably on the document. As a result, this new federal constitution became the law of the land. The people of Keene must have realized that they were commemorating a momentous occasion in the nation's history as they celebrated the new federal government more than 220 years ago.

Colonial Divorce

Divorce was very rare in colonial New Hampshire. The third divorce recorded in New Hampshire history was that of Greenwood and Sarah Carpenter of Swanzey in 1771.

Greenwood Carpenter petitioned the legislature asking that a law be enacted allowing him to divorce Sarah on the grounds of adultery. His petition indicated that he had joined in marriage with Sarah Leathers in 1752, with whom he had lived for eleven years and had several children. The petition went on to state that Sarah then voluntarily left him and the children, and after several years absence, she married another man, had a child by him and still remained in that relationship. Carpenter asked to be released from his marriage and be allowed to marry again.

Sarah was served with a copy of the petition and summoned to court but refused to appear. Consequently, in April 1771, the legislature passed an act discharging Greenwood Carpenter from the bonds of marriage and declaring that he could marry again as though Sarah were deceased. Carpenter then married Susan Hammond of Swanzey and began to rebuild his life.

That is not the end of the story, however. As a colony of England, the king had final say over the laws of New Hampshire. In December 1773, two and a half years after the legislature had approved the divorce, the king sent notice that he had disallowed the law dissolving the marriage. The legislature had no choice but to declare the divorce null and void. This late proclamation by the king apparently did not have much effect on the lives of Greenwood Carpenter and his new wife, Susan. Their first child was born ten months later in October 1774. They had nine more children over the next eighteen years. Greenwood Carpenter passed away in Swanzey in 1809.

Inventions, Discoveries, Business

The Briggs Washing Machine

The washing machine was one of the inventions that greatly eased the backbreaking workload of the housewife. All washing was necessarily done by hand before this invention. The town of Keene played a role in the development of this machine.

Keene resident Nathaniel Briggs placed an advertisement in a local newspaper concerning a washing machine that he had developed. He indicated that he believed that the most difficult part of housework was washing, a duty that was usually undertaken by the "Fair sex." Briggs advertised that most innovations have been made in favor of the male sex, but he felt that the "Fair sex" should receive the benefit of new innovations as well. Consequently, he had developed a washing machine that he felt would make the work of the housewife much easier. Briggs urged all the ladies to try his machine and not to feel obliged to wash by hand simply because their mothers had always done it that way. The date of this advertisement was June 27, 1797. Three months earlier, Briggs had received the first United States patent on a washing machine. Young Briggs, born shortly before the American Revolution, was a pioneer in the development of this important labor-saving device.

In 1859, the first rotary washing machine was invented, and the first all-electric machine was introduced in 1907. The all-important washing machine developed steadily and rapidly from this first patented machine, which Nathaniel Briggs was selling to the ladies of Keene more than two hundred years ago.

THE MARSH BROTHERS SEEK THEIR FORTUNES

Benjamin and Charles Marsh were born in Chesterfield, New Hampshire—Benjamin in 1823 and Charles in 1829. They were the sons of Reuben and Mary Marsh and the third generation of the family in Chesterfield. During the 1840s, the Marsh brothers headed for Boston to make their fortunes.

The brothers worked at separate jobs for a time. Charles was employed as a store clerk. In 1851, Benjamin joined with Eben Jordon to form a small dry goods store on Milk Street in Boston. They called the store Jordon Marsh & Company. Brother Charles joined the firm the following year. At the beginning they had only three clerks. Eben Jordon was allowed $1,200 a year for expenses because he was married. Each of the other partners was allowed $600 each year. They lived on that income for the first eight years. By that time, the store was doing $2 million worth of business annually, and they apparently felt that they could afford a bit more for living expenses.

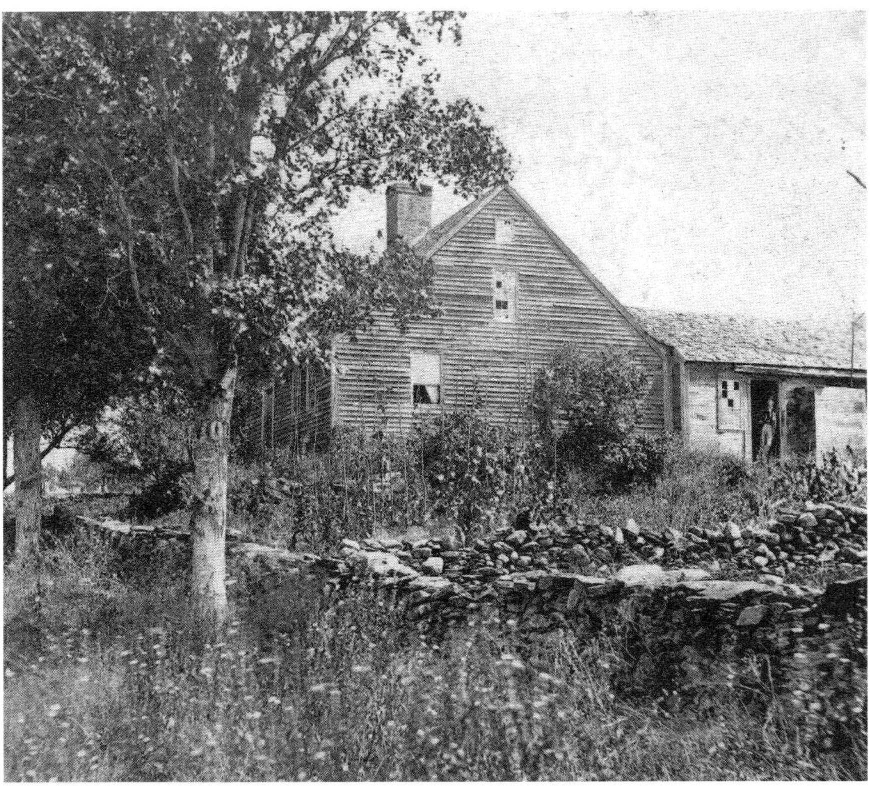

Childhood home of Benjamin and Charles Marsh in Chesterfield.

The firm continued to grow under the leadership of these men. Benjamin Marsh passed away in 1865 after nearly fifteen years as a partner in the firm. Charles Marsh continued with the firm for more than thirty years. By 1880, the company had become one of the largest retail firms in New England with six acres of retail space and nearly two thousand employees in a new retail store.

Today, Jordon Marsh continues as a large successful firm with retail stores throughout the region. It all began with the business genius of Eben Jordon and the Marsh brothers of Chesterfield.

Horace Wells and the Discovery of Anesthesia

Horace Wells was born in Hartford, Vermont, in January 1815. He spent a good portion of his youth in Cheshire County as a resident of Westmoreland. Wells attended the prestigious Chesterfield Academy and thereafter taught school in Westmoreland. During 1833 he studied dentistry under Dr. Stratton of Keene. Wells opened his own office in Hartford, Connecticut, in 1836.

From the beginning of his career, Wells was concerned with the pain caused during the extraction of teeth. He experimented with various narcotics, and by 1840, he felt that nitrous oxide might be an answer to the problem. It was not until 1844, however, that he experimented on himself with the gas. While under its influence, he had a tooth extracted from his own mouth without experiencing pain. Wells immediately began to use the gas on his patients. Other Hartford dentists soon followed suit. It was three years before anesthesia was attempted in Keene and first used by Wells's former teacher Dr. Stratton.

Wells traveled to Boston to share his discovery with others in his field, including Doctors T.G. Morton and Charles Jackson. In 1846, Doctors Morton and Jackson, who had been working on similar experiments, laid claim to the discovery of anesthesia and applied for a patent. Wells disputed their claim but to no avail. Morton and Jackson later submitted their claims to the Institute of France. Once again Wells disputed their claim, and once again he had no success. In 1847, Wells moved to New York and tried once again to further his own claim to the discovery. One year later, he was arrested on the charge that he had thrown sulfuric acid on a lady in the street. The arrest so aggravated his mental state that he committed suicide.

Wells was not forgotten, however, and was subsequently recognized as a pioneer in the field of anesthesia. The residents of Hartford erected a bronze statue in his memory. The statue of him still stands in Bushnell Park in Hartford, with an inscription that reads: "Horace Wells, the discoverer of anesthesia."

Taylor's Thermometers

George Taylor was born in a Stoddard, New Hampshire farmhouse in 1832. His grandfather had settled nearby and cleared the surrounding land forty years earlier. George spent his early years on the family farm, but as a teenager, he headed west to seek his fortune.

George Taylor stopped in Rochester, New York, where he met David Kendall, a young man whose father had been a pioneer thermometer maker. In 1851, Taylor, aged nineteen, and David Kendall pooled their resources, slightly more than $300, and began to manufacture thermometers on their own. The two men worked alone in one room over a drugstore. Kendall made the thermometer tubes, and Taylor handled the assembly, bookkeeping and sales. The firm moved to larger quarters within a few months, and the business expanded rapidly. The company soon began to produce barometers as well. Kendall left the firm in 1853, and Taylor continued on his own. Taylor's brother Frank later joined the firm, which became known as Taylor Brothers. The company continued to expand, new instruments were added to the line and Taylor thermometers were sold across the country. Three of George's sons joined the firm. One of them made the first sales trip to Europe, opening a world market.

Stoddard native George Taylor died in 1889, thirty-eight years after he made his first thermometer. His children and grandchildren continued his firm, which became known around the world as the Taylor Instrument Company.

Dr. Brewer and the Oil Industry

Francis Beattie Brewer was born in Keene in October 1820. As a young man, Brewer attended Dartmouth, from which he graduated in 1843 and earned a medical degree in 1846.

Dr. Brewer practiced medicine in Vermont and Massachusetts before moving to Titusville, Pennsylvania, in 1849. It was here that his interest and enthusiasm inspired the commercial use of oil. Dr. Brewer became involved in his father's lumber business there. He took an interest in an old oil spring on the company property that was being used as a source for lubricants.

Petroleum had been used for a variety of medical applications for centuries, and Dr. Brewer was interested in more widespread medical use. The lumber company took a lease on some land in 1853 with petroleum development in mind. Dr. Brewer convinced other doctors and scientists at New York and Dartmouth of the potential uses of petroleum. As a result, the Pennsylvania Rock Oil Company of New York was formed in 1854. The first oil well was erected and oil was struck in 1859.

Oil wells soon sprang up across the country, and many other uses were found for the oil being pumped from them. Dr. Francis Beattie Brewer moved on to other ventures, but the interest and enthusiasm of this Keene native had played a major role in the founding of one of this country's most important industries.

George Washington Snow and the Balloon Frame

George Washington Snow was born in Keene, New Hampshire, in September 1797. He left home as a young man and went to New York, where he found work as a carpenter and surveyor. He married while in New York and moved to Detroit with his wife.

In 1832, they moved farther west to Chicago, a town of 250 residents. The next year Chicago became a city, and Snow was made the first city assessor and surveyor. It was also during that year that Snow constructed a building that was to change the nature of house construction in America. That building was St. Mary's Church, the first building in America to be built with a balloon frame. The balloon frame involved the use of thin plates and studs running the entire height of the building and held together only by nails. Houses had previously been built with huge timbers held together with mortise and tenon joints.

Old-time carpenters laughed at the new style of construction. They said that the new frame was too weak and would collapse. They degraded the construction by calling it the balloon frame. The balloon frame proved very strong, however, and within two years, other carpenters were using it. By 1843, the balloon frame was being used all over the country. Two men could now accomplish what it had taken twenty men to do with the old-fashioned frame. The balloon frame also cut the cost of construction by 40 percent. Although he did not patent his invention, nor become wealthy from it, Keene native George Washington Snow revolutionized America's home construction industry.

JOSEPH GLIDDEN'S INVENTION

Joseph Glidden, son of David and Polly Glidden of Charlestown, New Hampshire, was born in that town in January 1813. Sixty years later, he patented an invention that changed the history of American agriculture. The Glidden family moved to New York when Joseph was still a boy. He spent several years on the family farm there and decided to become a farmer himself.

After graduating from college, he worked his way westward to Illinois by working for other farmers along the way. He bought a six-hundred-acre farm and settled down near DeKalb, Illinois. In 1873, Glidden attended a county fair, where he saw an exhibit of an early type of barbed wire. He thought he could make a better wire. In 1874, he patented a twisted wire that held the barbs in place. The following year Glidden formed the Barb Fence Company with a friend who invested $265 to become a half partner in the firm.

The new barbed wire was an immediate success, unlike other wires that had been designed before. Prior to that time, the Great Plains had been essentially unsettled because there was not enough timber there to build fences to control the roving herds of buffalo and cattle. With the use of Glidden's wire, farmers could protect their crops and ranchers could control their cattle.

One year after starting his Barb Fence Company, Glidden sold his half interest to a Worcester, Massachusetts company for $60,000, plus a large royalty. He soon became very wealthy. He bought several businesses in DeKalb, built the Glidden Hotel and bought 180,000 acres in Texas, where he kept fifteen thousand head of cattle. The barbed wire invented by Charlestown native Joseph Glidden opened the Great Plains to settlement and is recognized as one of the most important agricultural inventions in history.

Granite State Gold and Silver Mining Company

The town of Surry was once the scene of a substantial gold and silver mining operation. Surry Mountain was long thought to be the site of rich ore deposits, but it was not until 1879 that a company was incorporated for the purpose of mining in the area.

The Granite State Gold and Silver Mining Company was formed on September 15, 1879, with Mahlon Milleson as superintendent. The company's headquarters were located on Milk Street in Boston, and most of the officers were from that city. Prior to the formation of the company, Mr. Milleson, a mining engineer from Nevada, had been called in to give his opinion of the project. He was surprised to find ore that assayed at $190 per ton. Five hundred pounds of ore were taken to the Boston office to display as encouragement to potential stockholders.

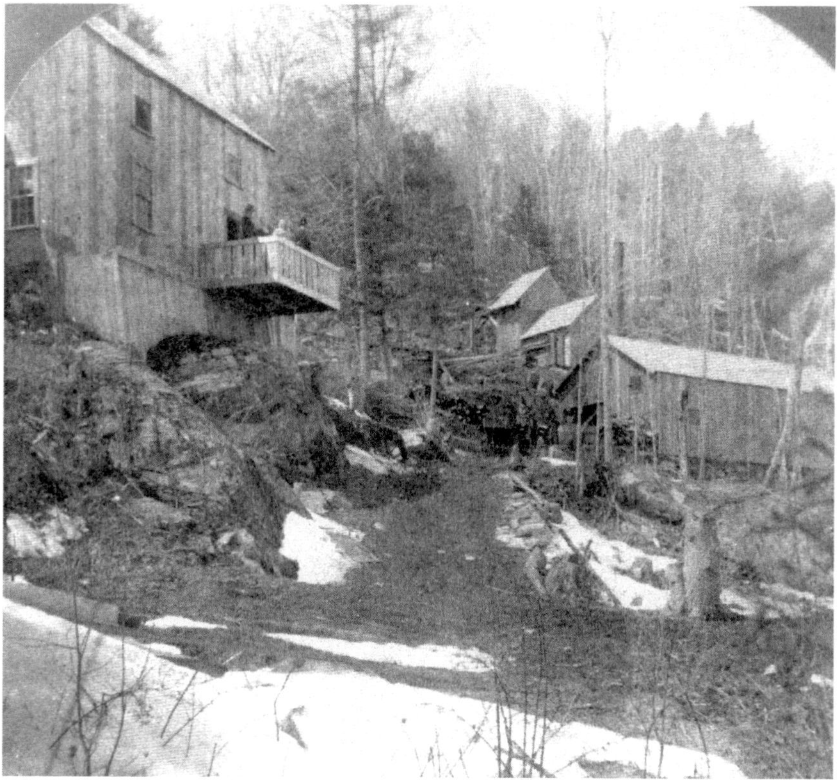

Buildings of the Granite State Gold and Silver Mining Company on Surry Mountain.

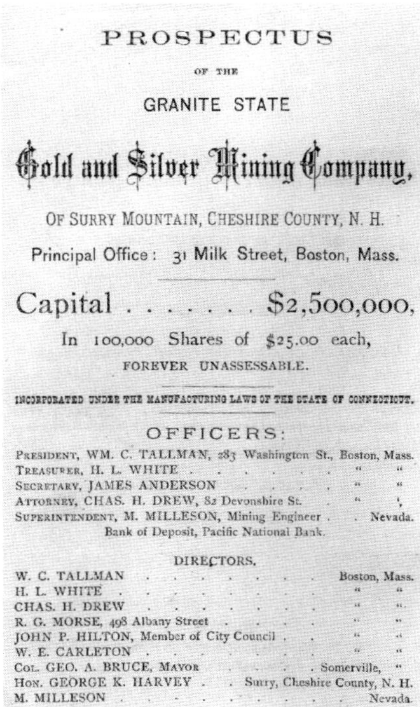

PROSPECTUS

OF THE

GRANITE STATE

Gold and Silver Mining Company,

OF SURRY MOUNTAIN, CHESHIRE COUNTY, N. H.

Principal Office: 31 Milk Street, Boston, Mass.

Capital $2,500,000,

In 100,000 Shares of $25.00 each,

FOREVER UNASSESSABLE.

INCORPORATED UNDER THE MANUFACTURING LAWS OF THE STATE OF CONNECTICUT.

OFFICERS:

President, WM. C. TALLMAN, 283 Washington St., Boston, Mass.
Treasurer, H. L. WHITE . . . . " "
Secretary, JAMES ANDERSON . . . . . " "
Attorney, CHAS. H. DREW, 82 Devonshire St. . " "
Superintendent, M. MILLESON, Mining Engineer . . Nevada.
Bank of Deposit, Pacific National Bank.

DIRECTORS.

W. C. TALLMAN . . . . Boston, Mass.
H. L. WHITE . . . . " "
CHAS. H. DREW . . . . " "
R. G. MORSE, 498 Albany Street . . . . . " "
JOHN P. HILTON, Member of City Council . . " "
W. E. CARLETON . . . . " "
Col. GEO. A. BRUCE, Mayor . . . . . Somerville, "
Hon. GEORGE K. HARVEY . . Surry, Cheshire County, N. H.
M. MILLESON . . . . Nevada.

Prospectus of the Granite State Gold and Silver Mining Company.

The company leased 175 acres on Surry Mountain, and a road was constructed running up to the mining site. A mill, manager's office and house and large boardinghouse for the workers were constructed. Full-time excavation began amidst great enthusiasm in 1880.

A second shaft was soon begun, and more buildings were constructed on the Gilsum side of the mountain. Ten or twelve men were employed for two or three years, but in the end, the enterprise proved unprofitable. The mining rights were sold at auction in February 1887 to pay back taxes, thus ending the experiment of the Granite State Gold and Silver Mining Company.

Roxbury's Professor Dolbear

Amos Emerson Dolbear was born in Norwich, Connecticut, in November 1837. He was orphaned at the age of four and came to Roxbury, New Hampshire, to live with Deacon Moses Guild. Dolbear attended the one-room district school in Roxbury and was noted as a quiet and studious youngster.

He later left Roxbury and worked his way through college as a schoolteacher. Dolbear graduated from Wesleyan University of Michigan the following year. He soon became professor of natural sciences at Bethany College in West Virginia. In addition to teaching, Dolbear served two terms as mayor of the city of Bethany. In 1874, he took a job as professor of physics and astronomy at Tufts College.

Professor Dolbear is best remembered as an inventor, however. Through his inventions he made great contributions to the advancement of science. Among his many inventions were the electrical gyroscope, writing telegraph, magneto telephone, static telephone, air space telegraph cable and a wireless telegraph. Dolbear also authored seven books and more than one hundred articles for scientific journals.

Despite his great success in the scientific community, Professor Amos Dolbear always retained his interest in his childhood home and continued to visit Roxbury until his death at the age of seventy-three.

Door-to-Door with Persis Albee

Persis Albee was a resident of Winchester during the early years of the twentieth century. She lived there with her children and operated a variety store on Depot Street.

During 1903, Mrs. Albee met Daniel McConnell, the founder of the California Perfume Company. Because of her retail experience, McConnell hired Albee as his first general agent. He gave her a sample case of his perfume and asked her to sell it throughout the town of Winchester. Mrs. Albee went door-to-door taking orders for the perfume from her neighbors. The perfume was a success, and she soon hired other workers to help with sales. The workers went from house to house selling the company's soaps and perfumes. They would send their orders into the company, and the products would soon arrive by Railway Express.

Other agents were hired, and the perfume was soon being sold across the country. Even today, Mrs. Albee is known as the mother of the company. In fact, the firm's highest award for sales achievement is known as the "Albee." The name of the company was changed to Avon, and the salespeople who came after Mrs. Albee were soon greeting women across the country with the words "Avon calling." Persis Albee's door-to-door sales in Winchester had launched one of the largest distributorships in the world.

Dog Biscuits

Carleton Ellis was born in Keene in 1876, the son of florist Marcus Ellis and his wife Katherine. Carleton received a camera as a present from his father on his twelfth birthday. The chemical reactions of photography fueled his imagination, and he soon began to experiment with chemicals. He became determined to enter the field of chemistry. He graduated as valedictorian of his high school class and went on to study at the Massachusetts Institute of Technology (MIT).

At age twenty-one, just after he graduated from college, Ellis invented paint remover. This began a long and distinguished career as an inventor. He moved to Montclair, New Jersey, and opened a laboratory there. Ellis's patents on his inventions soon numbered in the hundreds. His laboratories at Montclair eventually employed twenty assistants, all of them holding doctorate degrees.

During World War I, Ellis invented fireproof acetone to coat airplane wings for the military. He also invented moldable plastic to replace the more brittle celluloid, and in 1913, he patented the margarine we still use today. A form of margarine had been in existence for some years, but it had previously been made from animal fats. This animal fat margarine was greasy, often indigestible, and quite susceptible to contamination. Ellis's margarine, which could be made from either corn, peanut or cottonseed oil, was much safer and healthier than either animal fat margarine or the butter made from cow's milk at that time. As his number of inventions continued to climb, Ellis became known as the "second Edison."

The owner of a slaughterhouse once called on Ellis for his advice in disposing of the byproducts of his industry. Ellis's answer was an invention that earned him a fortune. From the byproducts he invented the dog biscuit. Inventor Carleton Ellis, "the miracle man of chemistry," died a millionaire in 1941. By that time, this Keene native held almost eight hundred patents, third in U.S. history, behind only Edison himself and scientist John O'Connor.

THE PORCH CHAIR CAPITAL

The manufacture of chairs for use in local homes was important in the early years of Keene, as it was in most large New Hampshire towns. By the late nineteenth century, however, local furniture companies were producing far more chairs than the local residents could use.

In 1870, there were two chair companies in Keene: the Cheshire Chair Company and the Keene Chair Company. These two firms employed

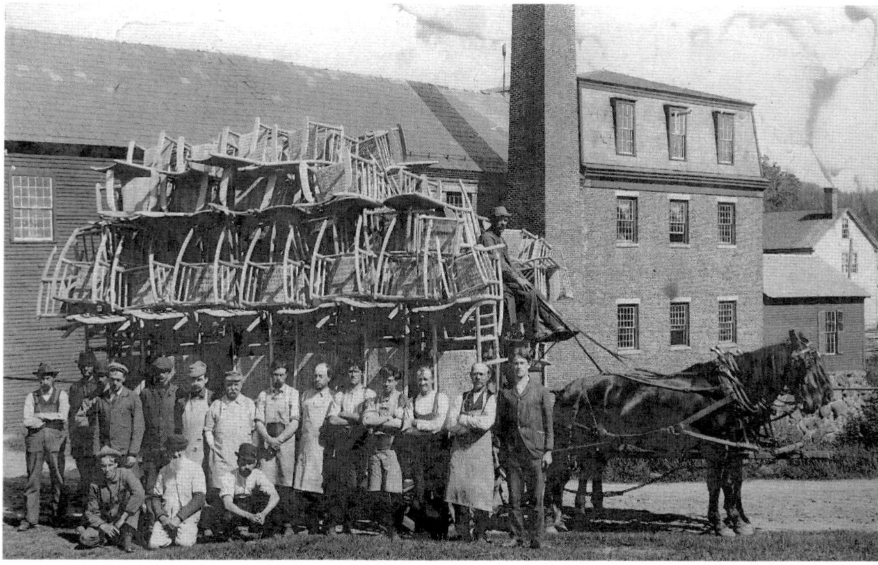

A load of porch rockers leaving the L.J. Colony Chair Company.

129 men who made 150,000 chairs that year. Many of those chairs were shipped out of town for sale in distant markets.

By the early twentieth century, there were six chair companies in Keene. The most popular product of these companies was the common porch chair, a simple straight back or rocking chair with a rattan seat. The six firms produced and shipped out approximately 1,000,000 chairs annually at that time; Keene became known as the "porch chair capital of the United States." The chairs were shipped by rail to markets across the country and to Europe.

A dozen chair companies came and went over the years. Keene's last porch chair producer, the Carey Chair Company, closed in 1963, ending this important chapter of the city's industrial history. Keene porch chairs are far from gone, however, as thousands still survive in homes across the United States.

Fame and Fortune

The Thomsonian System

Samuel Thomson was born in Alstead, New Hampshire, in 1769. He worked on his father's farm and attended local schools. He married in 1790 and soon thereafter purchased the family farm, which included land in Alstead and Surry, from his father.

Thomson and his wife, Susanna, soon began a family. Frequent illnesses within the family caused Thomson to convince a retired physician to move into a vacant house on the Thomson farm. In this way the doctor was nearby to attend to the family. Thomson became displeased with the doctor's treatment of one of his sons and dismissed him. Thomson then became his own family doctor, using herbal medicines that he made himself. He was so successful that he soon began to treat his neighbors as well. In 1806, Thomson left Cheshire County and eventually settled in Boston, where his fame grew.

He was one of the first men in America to oppose the methods used by the doctors of his day, such as bleeding and the use of what he called "poisonous medicines" such as mercury. He believed that all diseases resulted from improper body temperature. To maintain a proper temperature, he felt that all obstructions must be removed from the body's systems and that the process of digestion and natural perspiration must be working properly. His medical system was based on a simple cure of steam baths and herbal medicines to keep bodily functions working properly. He was ridiculed and called a quack by the doctors of his day, but he gained many followers. He

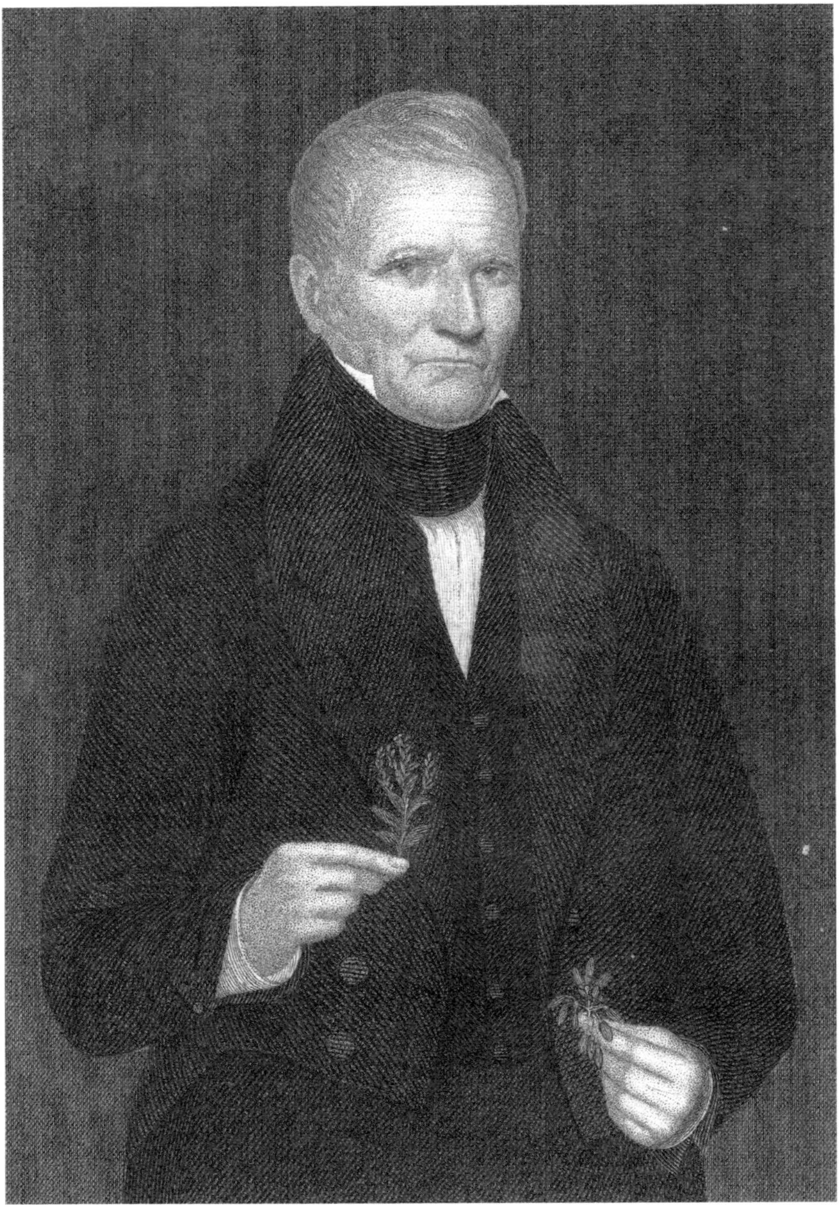

Dr. Samuel Thompson.

patented his medicines and his medical system and sold rights for their use at twenty dollars each. Despite the controversy over his methods, and the fact that he had no medical training, Samuel Thomson of Alstead gained fame and fortune from his "Thomsonian System of Medicine."

Little Women of Walpole

A young woman named Louisa moved to Walpole, New Hampshire, with her parents and three sisters in about 1850. It seems that Louisa's father, a philosopher and teacher, was somewhat down on his luck financially, and the family came to Walpole to stay with relatives. Young Louisa was about eighteen when they moved to Walpole, living with her aunt in Walpole village part time for several years.

During her years in Walpole, young Louisa spent much of her time helping with family work and working part time as a seamstress. She and her sisters acted in a local theatre, and Louisa took long walks about the village. Louisa also enjoyed writing and spent her spare time writing stories. A few of her stories were good enough for publication, and she began to earn a little extra income. After leaving Walpole, Louisa worked as a teacher and later became a volunteer nurse during the Civil War. In 1863, she wrote sketches of her experiences as a nurse. These were published and attracted considerable attention. In 1867, Louisa wrote a story that was partially based on her experiences in Walpole as a young woman. A local resident later stated that the story was a most accurate sketch of Louisa's early life in Walpole.

The story was published in 1868 and was an immediate success, selling eighty-seven thousand copies in three years. Louisa was soon famous and wealthy because of this story, with some of its elements drawn from her days in Cheshire County. Our young Louisa was Louisa May Alcott, and her story, entitled *Little Women*, is now known to millions of young people around the world.

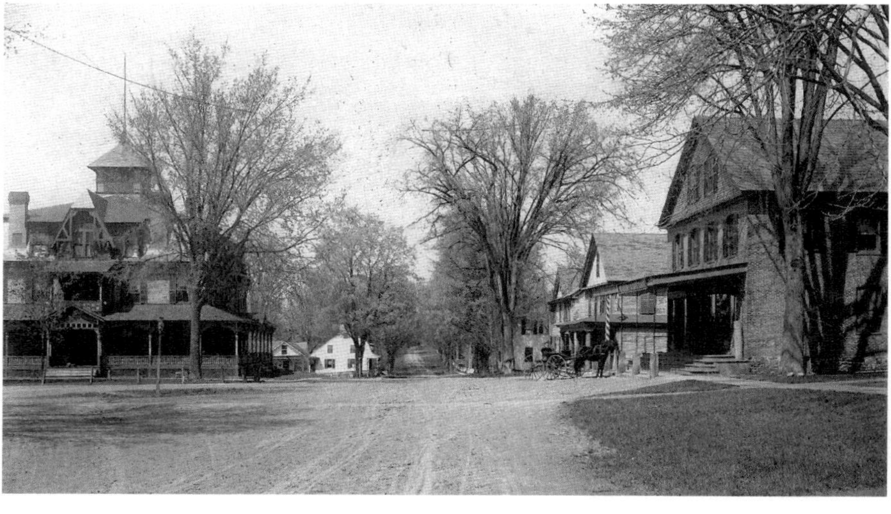

Main Street in Walpole, where Louisa May Alcott spent part of her youth.

Henry David

Many residents of the Monadnock region remember that Henry David's Restaurant, located on Keene's Main Street during the 1980s and 1990s, was named for famous author and naturalist Henry David Thoreau. But do you know why the restaurant was given that name?

In the 1780s, lawyer Asa Dunbar, his wife Mary and their four children lived there in the large white house on Keene's Main Street. The Dunbar's last child, Cynthia, was born there in May 1787. Exactly one month later, Asa Dunbar, the new baby's father, died. Asa's widow Mary opened her home as a tavern to support her young children, the oldest only fourteen years of age. Thus began the long history of this building for use as a tavern and restaurant.

Cynthia Dunbar grew up in the town before she married and moved to Concord, Massachusetts. In 1817, thirty years after her own birth in the large house on Keene's Main Street, Cynthia gave birth to a son—Henry David Thoreau.

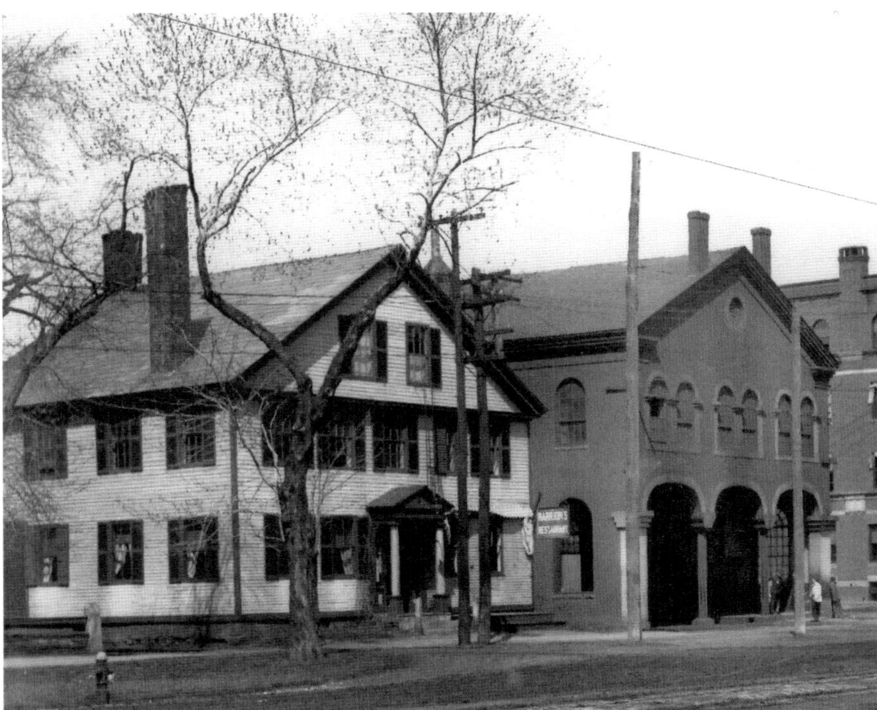

Childhood home of Cynthia Dunbar, on the left, and the Keene railroad station.

Thoreau was a frequent visitor to the region and was very familiar with Keene. He undoubtedly visited his grandmother, the widow Mary Dunbar, who outlived her husband by fifty years before she passed away in Keene in 1838. Thoreau described the region in detail in his writings. He often rode the train from his home in Massachusetts to the station at Troy. From there he would hike to Monadnock, camp on the mountain and record what he saw there in his journals.

In 1850, Henry David Thoreau wrote, "Keene Street strikes a traveler favorably, it is so wide, level, straight and long." One can picture him gazing down Keene's wide Main Street from a vantage point in front of the old home in which his mother was born sixty years earlier and that was for many years known as Henry David's Restaurant.

Trials and Tribulations of a Native Son

A baby boy was born to a farming family in Girard, Pennsylvania, in October 1833. His family moved to Swanzey, New Hampshire, in 1847 when he was fourteen years old. He attended school in Swanzey for three winter terms and worked with his father as a carpenter during the summer months.

Our subject left home at age seventeen to seek his fortune. He took a job as property boy with a circus in Boston and held several jobs during the next few years, including museum doorman, acrobat, stagehand and clerk in a dry goods store.

At age twenty-one he went to Toronto and played bit parts on stage for the next fourteen years. Our local boy quit the stage at age thirty-five, feeling that his career was going nowhere. He returned to the stage three years later, however, never making more than twenty-five dollars per week. He continued to act until an attack of rheumatism threatened his career.

It was during this illness, lying sick in a Pittsburgh hotel, that our native son conceived the idea of a short sketch based on his boyhood days in New Hampshire. He played the sketch in Pittsburgh; it was well received and became quite popular during the next few years.

In 1885, at the age of fifty-two, our gentleman decided to expand the sketch into a four-act play. The new play opened in Boston in April 1886. The name given to the play was *The Old Homestead*. The play's author, our

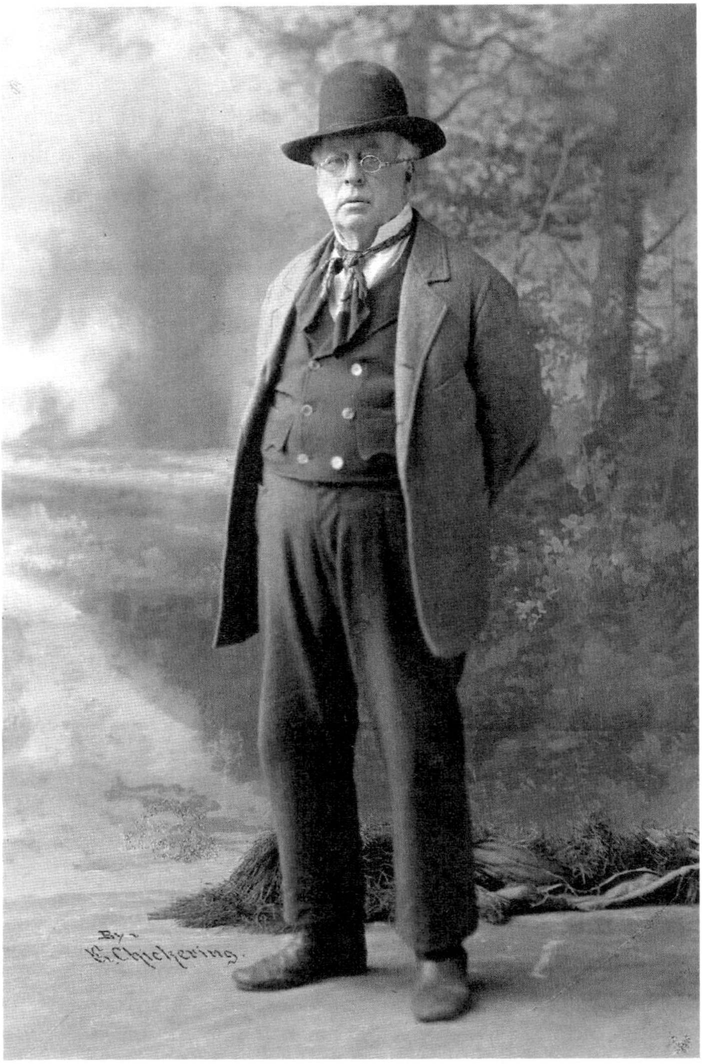

Denman Thompson as "Uncle Josh."

formerly obscure actor, was Swanzey's Denman Thompson. The play, based on Swanzey acquaintances from Thompson's youth, became one of the most successful in the nation's history and played throughout the United States for the next twenty-five years, with Thompson playing the lead role of Uncle Josh. Our obscure actor, Denman Thompson, retired to Swanzey a wealthy playwright, leaving behind a play that continues to delight audiences to the present day.

Travel and Transportation

The First Connecticut River Bridge

Prior to the 1780s, there were no bridges spanning the Connecticut River. Colonel Enoch Hale was determined to build such a bridge despite the scornful laughter of the many people who said that it could not be done.

Colonel Hale, a well-known and prosperous citizen of Rindge, petitioned the New Hampshire legislature for the right to build and operate a toll bridge between Walpole and Bellows Falls. He was granted a charter for construction in December 1783. Hale soon moved to Walpole and began construction. The process was long and difficult—one young worker died when he fell from the bridge to the rocks below.

Hale's Connecticut River Bridge was completed in 1785. This was the very first bridge to span the Connecticut River and remained the only bridge on the river until 1796. The legislature set the rate of tolls at three cents for each person on foot, six cents for a horse and rider and twelve and a half cents for a horse and wagon.

The bridge was acclaimed to "exceed any ever built in America in strength, elegance, and public utility." It is still considered one of America's most outstanding bridge constructions of the eighteenth century.

The Connecticut River Bridge carried passengers for many years. It was eventually found to be weakened from decay, and a new bridge was built upriver. When the new bridge was completed, Colonel Hale's great engineering landmark, the first bridge over the Connecticut, was cut down and carried away by the waters of the river.

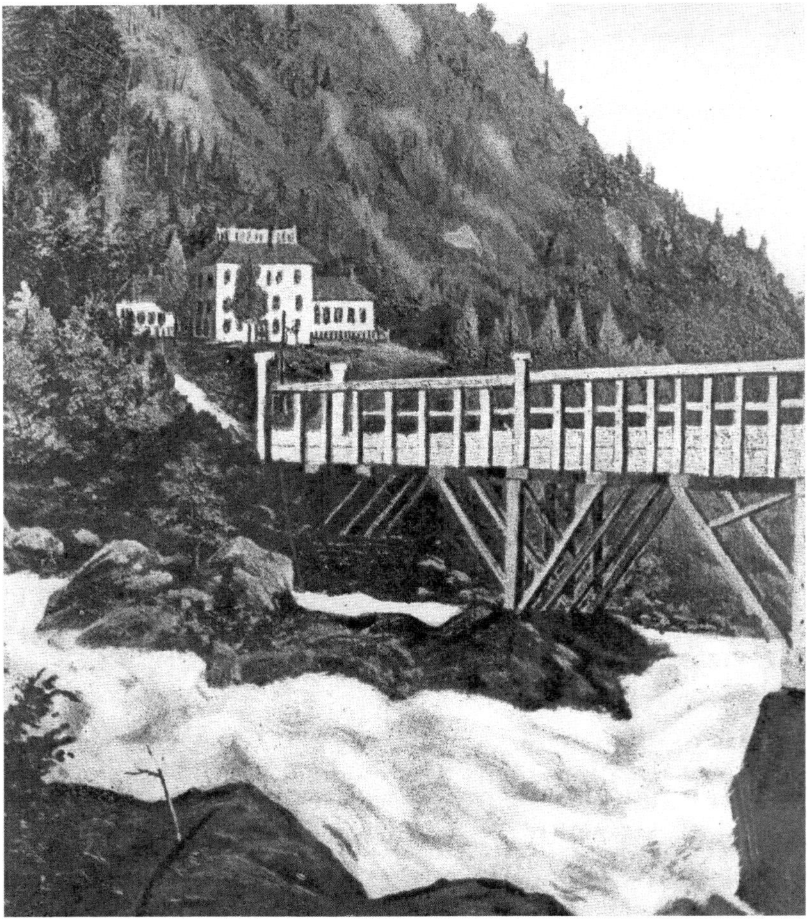

The Connecticut River Bridge over the falls between Walpole and Bellows Falls.

THE BELLOWS FALLS CANAL

The village of Bellows Falls, located across the Connecticut River from Walpole, New Hampshire, was the site of an important eighteenth-century engineering project, the construction of one of the first canals in the United States.

The Vermont state legislature chartered the canal in October 1792. The purpose of the canal was to allow for navigation around the impassable

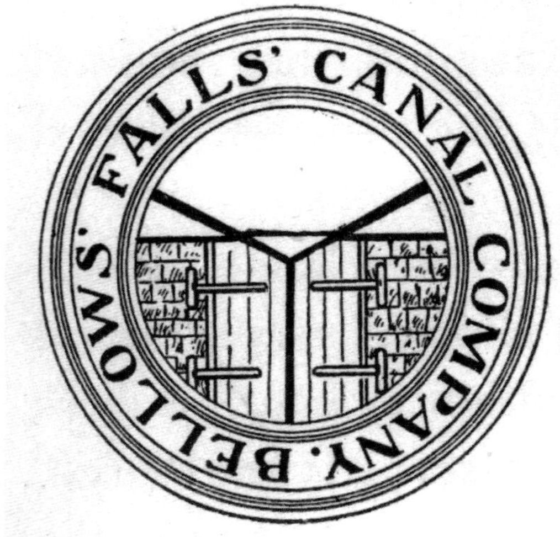

Bellows Falls' Canal Company corporate seal.

channel and dangerous falls. Three brothers of the Atkinson family of London were granted exclusive rights to build the canal and erect a dam across the river.

The work proved difficult, and the construction of the canal required ten years to complete. By the time the first boat passed through the canal in 1802, the Atkinson brothers had spent $105,000 to build the dam, canal and locks.

This was one of a series of six canals built on the river to allow for the continuous movement of freight and passengers along the waterway. The canal was a busy place. During the year of 1828, 103 boats weighing more than seven thousand tons passed through the canal.

The development of railroads and improved highways after 1850 was the beginning of the end for the river's canal system. The Atkinson family sold the canal to two Keene men in 1866, and it was used mainly for water power for local mills after that time. The dam and canal were rebuilt for hydroelectric purposes between 1926 and 1928, and the old Bellows Falls Canal became a footnote in Connecticut River history.

Navigation on the Ashuelot River

Of the thousands of people who daily cross the Ashuelot River over the bridge on West Street in Keene, nearly all of them would be astounded to realize that almost two hundred years ago the river was considered practical for navigation.

Yet on June 24, 1819, the New Hampshire legislature passed an act that granted to Lewis Page the sole authority to clear, deepen and straighten the Ashuelot River from the Faulkner & Colony Mill to the river's junction with the Connecticut River, as well as to make dams, locks and canals where necessary.

The legislature authorized a toll not to exceed fifty cents per ton transported between Keene and the dam at Winchester, a distance of about seventeen miles, and a similar toll from the Winchester dam to the Connecticut River.

Many people subscribed liberally to the project. Two locks were built, one at Whitcomb's Mill and one at Emerson's Mill, in Swanzey.

On November 19, 1819, the first boat, the *Enterprise*, sixty feet long and capable of carrying fifteen to twenty tons, arrived at Keene from Winchester. Many residents made the maiden voyage aboard the *Enterprise* and celebrated on their arrival at Keene.

The *Sentinel* covered the event, questioning whether the project would be a financial success. The reporter stated that

> *with the exception of three miles land carriage, the productions of all parts of the world may now be brought to our doors by water, and by the same channel, our lumber and produce may go to the ocean. The benefits to be derived will soon be tested by experience…and due notice will be hereafter given on the arrival at this port of the first steamboat from Hartford or New York.*

This steamboat never arrived, however, as the project failed to meet the expectations of its sponsors and was soon abandoned.

Although the question of navigating the river remained a concern for several years, the arrival and overwhelming success of the railroad thirty years later ended the idea of transporting products on the Ashuelot forever.

STEAMBOATS ON THE RIVER

We picture Mark Twain and colorful tales of the Mississippi when we think about steamboats, but the Connecticut River was also navigated by steamers for more than a century. The 1820s and 1830s were the golden age of steam navigation on that portion of the river, which borders the Monadnock region. Canals were built around dams and rapids, including one of the earliest canals in the country at Bellows Falls, and boats would steam up to that point and beyond carrying products and passengers.

One of the most colorful local steamboat stories involved a boat called the *William Hall*—a stern wheeler, probably seventy or eighty feet long. This boat was built in 1831 and soon made a trial run up the river and arrived at Bellows Falls. The locks of the Bellows Falls Canal were only about twenty feet wide, however, and the *William Hall* simply would not fit into the canal. The captain was not defeated, though. He docked his boat at the lower landing at Bellows Falls and hired eight teams of oxen. The oxen pulled the boat out of the river, up Mill Street, through the Square and up Canal Street to the upper landing. The *William Hall* must have been an amazing sight rolling through the streets of the village. The steamer was launched at the upper landing and continued north. Farther upriver at Hartland, Vermont, the steamer once again was too wide for the locks. The *William Hall* turned around and sailed back downriver. Once again the oxen hauled the boat through the streets of Bellows Falls, and the ship started the voyage back to Hartford.

The *William Hall* never went through Bellows Falls again, and it wasn't long before all of the steamers stopped coming to the village. The railroad had arrived in the region, and the upper Connecticut steamboat era soon came to a close.

Rufus Porter and the Airship

Rufus Porter is best remembered today for his work as an itinerant artist. He painted wall murals in more than one hundred homes throughout New England between 1815 and 1840. Porter was also a scientist, however. He invented a life preserver, a fire alarm system, a washing machine and a revolving rifle, which he sold to Samuel Colt.

Porter painted murals on the walls of more than a dozen Monadnock region homes—in Jaffrey, Langdon, Hancock and other local towns—in the 1820s. Perhaps during his time in our region he spent his evenings sketching and planning his most amazing invention. It was during this decade that Rufus Porter designed an airship very similar to the lighter-than-air vehicles that were actually flying one century later. It was not until the late 1840s that he published his plan and tried to build the airship. The vehicle was to be powered by steam and would carry up to one hundred passengers at a speed of sixty to one hundred miles per hour. A three-day flight was planned from New York to San Francisco in 1849; the ticket price of fifty dollars would include meals.

Porter built scale models that performed perfectly, but he could not raise the funds for the airship itself. He petitioned the Senate for $5,000, but the petition was referred to committee and was not seen again. He finally formed a stock company and sold six hundred shares at $5 each to raise funds to build the ship. Following many setbacks, the full-scale model was built but never got off the ground. Thus ended the dream of Rufus Porter, who had looked to the sky as he walked the roads of New Hampshire forty years earlier and imagined an easier way to travel from one mural painting job to another.

THE COLD RIVER DISASTER

Early on the morning of March 14, 1837, a northbound stagecoach left the village of Walpole. When the coach reached Cold River, it was found that recent rains had swollen the river so that water and ice were passing dangerously close to the bridge there.

The coach was carrying five passengers. Three of these were women, including two sisters who were traveling to Cornish to visit their sick mother, and a Mrs. Dunham who was returning home to Woodstock from the Lowell mills at which she had been working. The men were Chipman Swain, a pension agent who was carrying $1,500 in a small trunk, and a traveler by the name of Wilson.

Stage driver William Simonds slowed his horses to a walk and proceeded across the bridge. As the coach neared the opposite shore, the bridge collapsed, sending it and the stage into the swirling, ice-filled water. Simonds and Mr. Wilson jumped from their seats on top of the stage. Wilson quickly reached the shore, and Simonds clung to branches near the mouth of Cold River. Mr. Swain and Mrs. Dunham clung to each other as they were swept into the Connecticut River. Swain tried desperately to pull Mrs. Dunham from the water. He did not succeed, however, and she was crushed by the huge blocks of ice. Swain stayed by her side until her death and then made his way toward the shore. Along the way he found his trunk of pension money, retrieved it and climbed onto the bank of the river.

The bridge and the coach were broken into small pieces by the swirling ice at the mouth of Cold River. The sisters from Cornish were not seen again after the bridge collapsed, and their bodies were not recovered until the following summer. The driver was pulled from the water by townspeople who came to the rescue, but it was too late to save the three female passengers. Three of the four horses also perished. The Cold River disaster was probably the worst stagecoach accident in the history of the region.

Stoddard's Stone Arch Bridge

Near the Stoddard/Antrim town line, beside New Hampshire highway Route 9, stands a twin-arch highway bridge made of stone. This bridge was built without any mortar and is sustained solely by the shaping of its arch stones. It is one of several surviving bridges of this unique style that were constructed primarily in the Contoocook River Valley in the first half of the nineteenth century. Today this bridge, and others like it, has received national recognition for its contribution to our country's civil engineering heritage. The stone arch bridge in Stoddard was not always appreciated as much as it is today, however.

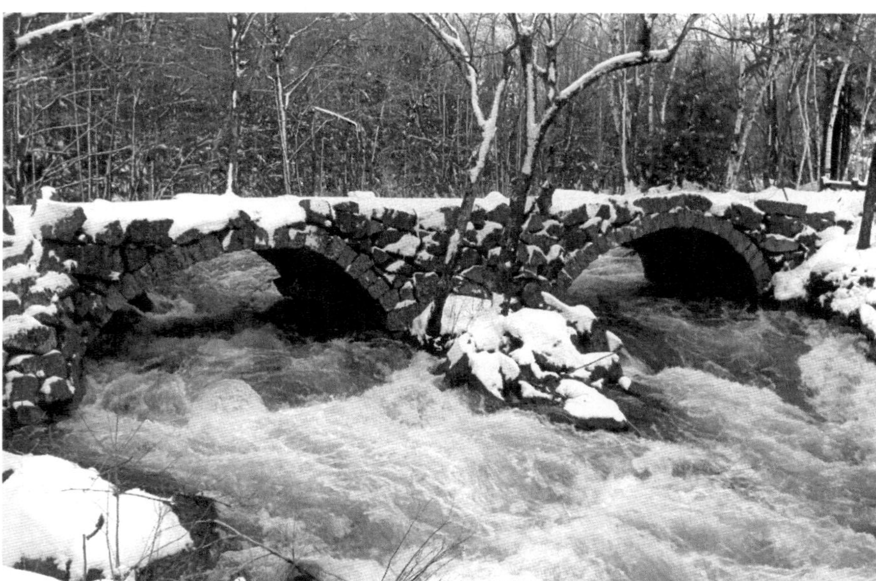

Stoddard's stone arch bridge.

At the town meeting in March 1852, the residents of Stoddard voted to build a new bridge over the North Branch River on the road to Antrim. The town's three selectmen, Abner Knowlton, Nathan Morse and William Wilson, would oversee the project. The bridge that the selectmen contracted and paid for with town funds was this stone arch bridge, which still stands near Stoddard's eastern boundary.

The town's residents became very upset when they saw the bridge being constructed, however. They felt that the twin-arch bridge was much too extravagant and a waste of the taxpayer's money. Despite their objections, the bridge was completed and put into use. The taxpayers had the last word, however, as they would never again elect the three selectmen under whose direction the structure had been built. Little did those Stoddard residents realize that the bridge they had condemned would survive for more than 150 years to be recognized as a landmark of American engineering.

HINSDALE'S AUTO PIONEER

In 1875, one of the earliest automobiles in the United States was built in Hinsdale, New Hampshire. George Long, the inventor of this auto, was a resident of Northfield, Massachusetts. A proper workshop was not available in Northfield, however, so Long came to New Hampshire, where he worked on his project in the machine shop of Holman and Merriman in downtown Hinsdale.

Long got the idea for his auto from a three-wheel vehicle that he had seen at a fair in Brattleboro in 1862. After experimenting for some time with

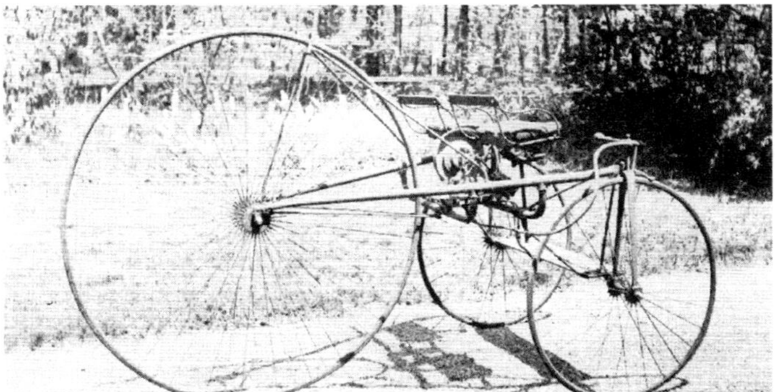

An early automobile built by George Long in 1882.

kerosene, powdered coal and gunpowder, he finally discovered that charcoal was the best fuel to fire the steam boiler that would power his vehicle.

Long's vehicle had a bicycle-type frame, wooden wheels and a driving gear in the rear axle. It could travel thirty miles per hour, roads permitting, which they seldom were.

When Long drove his auto into Northfield, he was ordered to "take it off the streets as it scared horses, astounded citizens and was considered a menace to public safety." Despite this discouragement, Long continued to drive his early auto but was forced to travel the back roads at night to avoid detection. He also continued his experimenting and later patented one of the first gasoline automobiles, which now resides in the Smithsonian Institution.

The Hog Train Wreck

On July 17, 1897, a freight train left the Bellows Falls station at 10:33 a.m. en route to Boston. The train, pulled by two locomotives and trailed by a caboose, consisted of twenty-three freight cars full of live hogs. Milan Curtis was the engineer of the lead locomotive; Mr. Hagar was the engineer of the second locomotive.

The train reached the Summit at Westmoreland and began the descent into the city of Keene. It was travelling at a speed of thirty to thirty-five miles per hour. As it rounded a curve near the stone arch on Arch Street, about two miles west of the railroad station on Main Street, the front locomotive suddenly left the track. Mr. Curtis whistled for brakes, and then he and his fireman sprang from their seats and were immediately thrown from the locomotive. Mr. Hagar, in the second locomotive, applied the brakes, but it was already too late. His engine had already left the tracks as well. He and his fireman jumped or were thrown out of the engine. The two locomotives and the first five freight cars were immediately piled into a mass of shattered debris. Milan Curtis was killed and Mr. Hagar was seriously injured, but the rest of the train crew escaped with minor injuries. Many hogs were killed, and others wandered off into the surrounding woods and fields.

The New Hampshire Board of Railroad Commissioners investigated the accident. The track and the train were in perfect repair, and there was no

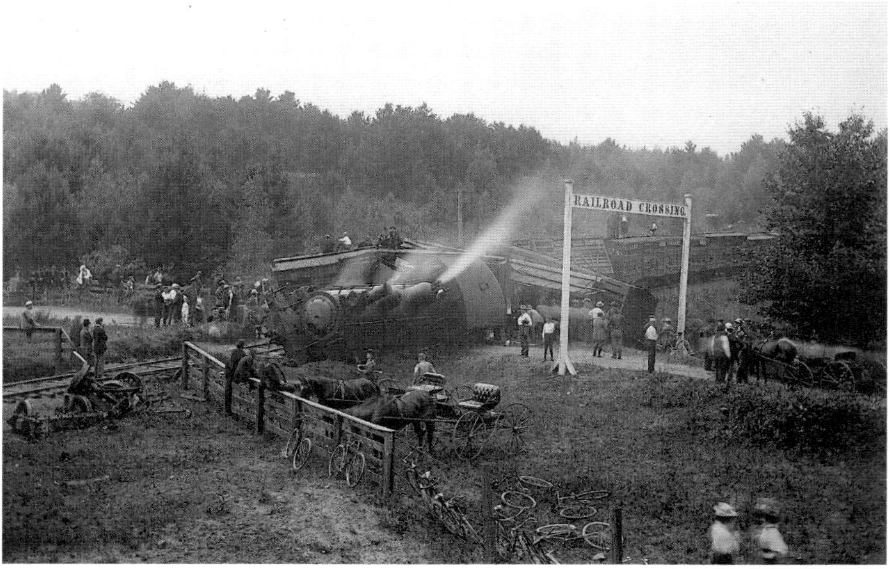

The wreck of the twenty-three-car hog train in West Keene in 1897.

warning of danger. About two hours after the accident, however, a broken piece of three-fourths-inch track bolt was found alongside the rails. It was flattened and battered as if it had recently been run over by an engine. It was determined that this bolt was probably the cause of the derailment. It was never determined how the bolt may have come to be on the tracks, if by human hand or other means.

The wreck drew a large crowd of curious onlookers and is still attracting attention today more than a century later. Stonewall Farm, located near the site of the wreck, commemorated the incident with special events on the 100th anniversary of the accident.

TRINITY CYCLE COMPANY

The Trinity Cycle Manufacturing Company factory on Railroad Street in Keene was dedicated on November 11, 1897. Bicycles were extremely popular for recreation and transportation at that time, and the Trinity Company had well over one hundred employees by the time it unveiled its new models in February 1898.

Frank Fowler, the firm's first president, was soon replaced by local attorney Alfred T. Batchelder. Arthur Faulkner served as treasurer. Many local furniture makers took jobs in this new industry. By March they were turning out thirty bicycles each day. These "wheels," as they were commonly called at the time, sold for about twenty-eight dollars retail. Business reports indicated that the Trinity was a first-class bicycle. The firm soon employed 150 people and increased production to forty cycles per day.

Trinity built a strong reputation and gained a large following. During the spring of 1899, the plant operated until 9:00 p.m. daily in an attempt to turn out sixty bicycles per day. The crew still could not keep up with the orders coming in.

Although business was good, the resignation of W.H. Little in 1899 was a sign of things to come. He left to take a position with the Locomobile Company of Westboro, Massachusetts, builders of motor carriages. The Trinity Company sent three salesmen out across the country in December, shipped new bicycles all winter long and worked long hours throughout the 1900 season.

This was a time of rapid change in the transportation industry, however. That change came to the Trinity Company. Plant superintendent Reynold Janney was building an automobile at the factory. He perfected the car during the early months of 1900, and the company began to manufacture autos in July of that year. Seven months later, the Trinity Cycle Company was superseded by the Steamobile Company of America, and car manufacture replaced bicycle manufacture on Railroad Street in Keene.

The Steamobile Company of America

In the early days of the auto industry, it was not unusual for small firms to produce cars in small towns throughout the country. Keene was the home of one such company. Reynold Janney built an experimental auto in the Trinity Cycle Manufacturing Company plant on Church Street in 1900. Janney was the superintendent of this bicycle factory that was housed in the Jones Building, where auto dealerships were later located. The experimental machine, a light pleasure wagon, was given its trial run on June 26, 1900. The car had three cylinders attached to a revolving shaft. The shaft activated gears that powered the vehicle. Steam power was used to run the engine.

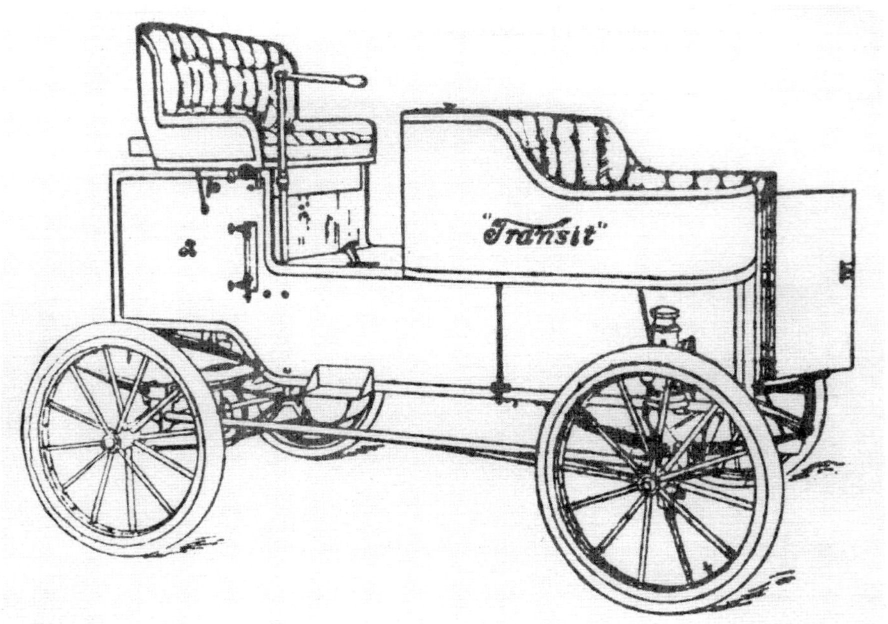

The Transit, built by the Steamobile Company of America.

The trial run was successful, and in January 1901 the Church Street factory began production of the Runabout. During the next month the *Keene Sentinel* announced that the Steamobile Company of America, a Delaware corporation with capital stock of $500,000, had acquired the factory, machinery and patent rights of the Trinity Cycle Company and was to commence the manufacture of the new auto under the name "Steamobile." The new firm was to test the model built the previous summer and then begin work on 125 of the new vehicles. At least 25 Runabouts were sold by September, and a second model was introduced the next month.

During February 1902, a third model, the Transit, was introduced. The Transit could carry up to seven passengers, or the passenger compartment could be removed and a freight carrier substituted, making it a delivery wagon. The new model went from design to road testing in sixteen days. It could be powered by steam, gasoline or electricity. The price of the company's three models ranged from $850 to $1,000.

Despite its early success, the Steamobile Company of America was out of business by June 1902. During that month all assets of the firm, including forty unsold autos, were sold to the Standard Roller Bearing Company of Philadelphia. Illustrations of these early Steamobiles are all that remain of Keene's brief entry in the nation's automobile industry.

The Widest Paved Main Street in the World

Many of us have seen postcards of Keene's Main Street overprinted with the words "The Widest Paved Main Street in the World." The development of this unique street can be traced to a single day in the autumn of 1736, just two years after the first settlers arrived in the town.

A meeting of the proprietors of the township was held on the October 1, 1736, at the log home of Nathan Blake on the corner of what later became Winchester and Main Streets. The settlers voted at that meeting to double the width of the town's Main Street from four rods to eight rods because "the Town Street is judged too narrow conveniently to accommodate the Proprietors." The land owners surrendered four rods of their property on the street and were given four rods on the rear of their lots as repayment.

The street was widened from 66 to 132 feet, thus establishing the character of the village that local residents have enjoyed ever since. The settlers did not record why a 66-foot-wide street was not "conveniently" wide enough in a thick forest with only a few footpaths and one or two permanent homes. Whatever their motives might have been, however, we owe a debt of gratitude to these early settlers for their foresight in laying out this attractive Main Street, which we still enjoy today.

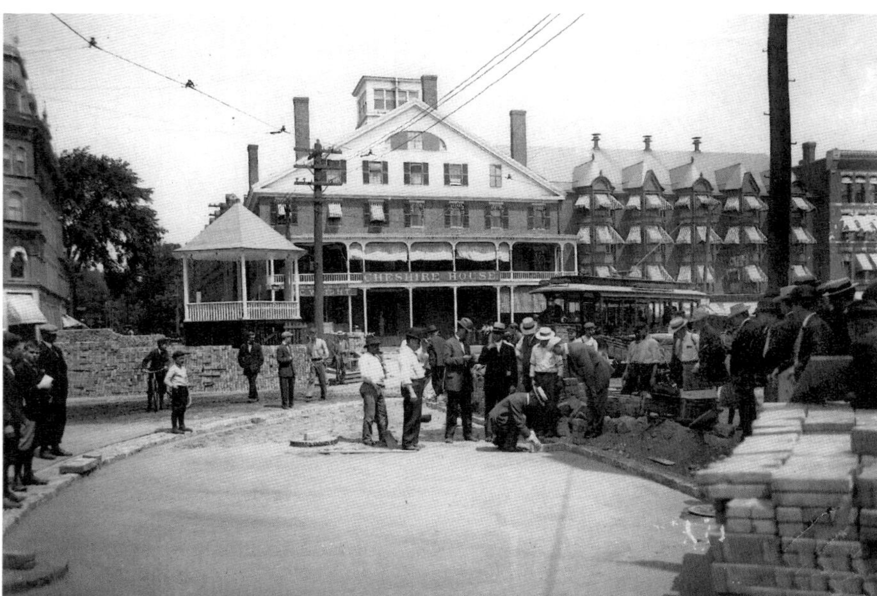

Placing the first paving blocks on the "Widest Paved Main Street in the World," 1910.

A Message from the Sky

On the morning of July 27, 1927, the faint sound of an engine was heard in the sky above Keene. The sound grew louder, and a small airplane appeared over the city. The plane circled above Keene several times, and then, at 11:10 a.m., Charles A. Lindbergh reached out of the *Spirit of St. Louis* and dropped a large parchment down into the city. Lindbergh flew out of sight. John Rule of Keene picked up the document, a greeting to the city, and presented it to city officials.

Lindbergh had made his famous solo flight from New York to Paris two months earlier. He became a national hero and soon undertook a promotional tour to encourage commercial aviation. His fly-by and hand-delivered greetings were the extent of his visit to Keene during the tour.

A portion of the greeting read as follows: "To the city of Keene. We wish to send you this greeting from the air to express our sincere appreciation of your interest in the tour and in the promotion and expansion of commercial aeronautics in the United States."

Lindbergh's solo flight and visit to Keene undoubtedly fueled the thoughts of several Keene residents who were already interested in aviation. Keene's first airport was opened fourteen months later in September 1928.

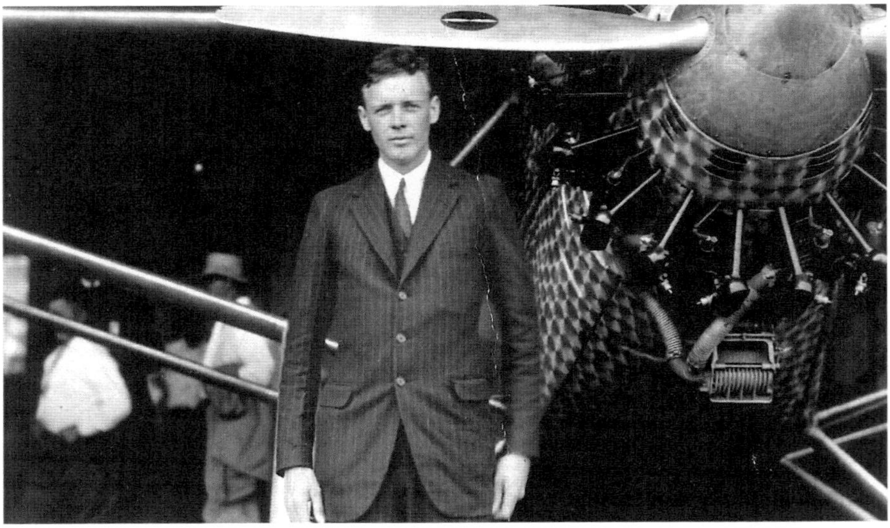

Charles Lindbergh and the *Spirit of St. Louis* at Concord, New Hampshire.

Politics

Peleg Sprague, Congressman

Peleg Sprague was the first of several Keene residents to serve as a United States Congressman and the eighth New Hampshire resident elected to the U.S. Congress.

Sprague was born in Rochester, Massachusetts, in 1756. He graduated from Dartmouth in 1783; studied law in Charlestown, New Hampshire; and was admitted to the bar in 1785. Sprague moved to Keene two years later to practice law. In 1797, he was elected to Congress and soon traveled to Philadelphia, the seat of government at that time.

Six letters from Congressman Sprague in Philadelphia to his wife, Rosalinda, in Keene have survived. These letters give us a glimpse of a way of life much different from ours today. Transportation, for example, was quite different. When Sprague arrived in Philadelphia, he wrote that "[t]he stages from Walpole to Springfield were so slow that I never got to Hartford til Thursday night…Don't you think it pretty quick traveling to go 230 miles in…48 hours? I never slept but 6 hours in 3 nights, and when I got to this city I was weary and very dirty."

Sprague also described fashions in the city. The latest fashion was for the ladies, young and old, to shave their heads and wear colored wigs. He stated that red wigs were the most fashionable, but that blue ones were nearly as popular.

Most of all, however, Sprague told Rosalinda how much he missed her and that he longed to be with her and their children. On February 4, 1799, he wrote, "This is the last letter I expect to write to you from this city during this session of Congress—Thank God it will [close] next Saturday, and then I shall set my face homeward with joy."

Sprague returned to Keene and was reelected to Congress for a second term in 1799. He refused to serve, however, due to ill health. Peleg Sprague passed away in the spring of the following year at the age of forty-three.

ELIZA BALLOU OF RICHMOND

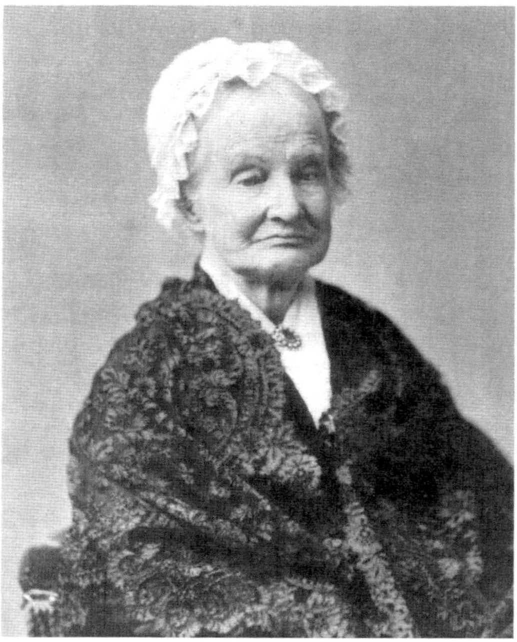

Eliza Ballou Garfield.

The Ballou family was among the earliest settlers of the town of Richmond at the southern border of Cheshire County. Twelve-year-old James Ballou came to Richmond in 1773 with his parents and several brothers and sisters. James grew up in Richmond, married Mehitable Ingalls, the town clerk's daughter, and built a home and farm near his father's home. In 1803, he moved to a house near the Richmond Four Corners, where he opened a store. James attained considerable local prominence for his ability to foretell the future and locate missing property.

James and Mehitable's sixth child, Elizabeth, better known as Eliza, was born in September 1801. Eliza spent her early childhood years in Richmond. James Ballou died in 1808, and Mehitable took her children and went to join her father, who was now living in Worcester, New York. Eliza passed the remainder of her youth there.

She later married Abram Garfield, and they settled on the Ohio frontier in 1830. Abram had barely made a beginning for the family in Ohio when he died following a sudden illness. Eliza was left with four small children, the youngest of whom was an infant son. She brought up the children unaided in the poverty of her isolated log cabin. It was the youngest son who accompanied his mother on a visit to her childhood home in Richmond many years later. This youngest son of Eliza Ballou Garfield of Richmond, New Hampshire, was James A. Garfield, future Civil War general and twentieth president of the United States.

Ithamar Chase's Son

Ithamar Chase was a resident of Cornish, New Hampshire, when he married Janette Ralston of Keene in 1792. Janette was the daughter of Alexander Ralston, owner of the Ralston Tavern in Keene. Shortly after the death of Ralston in 1810, the Chases, with their several children, moved to Keene so that Ithamar could operate the tavern.

One of their sons was called Salmon, named after an uncle. This young boy first attended school in Keene in what he called "a dark room on Main Street." He later studied under the Reverend Zedekiah Barstow at the old Wyman Tavern. Barstow later recalled that young Chase was a raw and uncouth lad but very talented and an apt scholar.

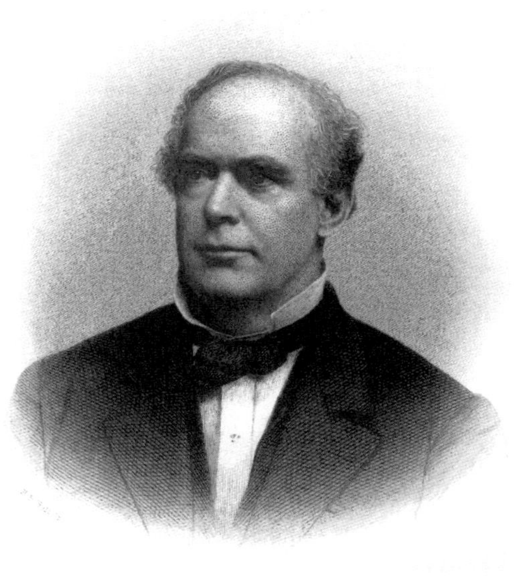

Salmon P. Chase.

Ithamar Chase invested his wife's inheritance into Keene's glass industry. The glass business failed, and Ithamar Chase died in 1817, leaving the family quite poor. Consequently, the Chases' young son went to Ohio to live with his uncle in 1820. He returned to Keene in 1823 at the age of fifteen. Chase taught school in Roxbury for a short time and then went on to study at Dartmouth, from which he graduated in

1826. Following graduation, he went to Washington, D.C., to study law and opened a practice in Cincinnati four years later.

From his humble beginnings in Keene, Salmon P. Chase went on to become a United States senator, governor of Ohio, secretary of the treasury, chief justice of the Supreme Court and one of the most distinguished statesmen of his day.

DANIEL WEBSTER IN KEENE

New Hampshire native Daniel Webster was well known to the residents of Cheshire County during the first half of the nineteenth century. He had argued cases in the court at Keene as a young lawyer. By the time of the presidential election of 1840, however, he had become a national political figure who had served several terms in the U.S. House and Senate. He was also recognized as one of the greatest public speakers in the nation. The people of the region were thrilled to hear that he would stop in Keene on his campaign tour in support of the Whig presidential candidate William Henry Harrison.

On the morning of July 9, the day of the speech, large crowds began to converge on Keene. The haying was completed in the countryside, and farmers and their families came into town. They were joined by businessmen, laborers, housewives and children from Keene. A huge platform had been built for the speakers near the Keene Academy building on Winter Street. By the time Webster took the stand at 2:30 p.m., the audience had grown to four thousand people. The great orator spoke for two hours. The huge audience was silent throughout the speech so that every word could be heard. At one point, a support gave way and the platform settled several inches. Webster proclaimed that "if the Whig platform goes down, I go with it" and continued his speech. By the time he finished, the sun was low in the western sky. That evening Webster was honored at a reception at General Wilson's mansion on Main Street.

Weeks later, Harrison was indeed elected, but many who had been present on Winter Street that day felt that it should be Daniel Webster himself who should be next president of the United States.

The Governors Dinsmoor

Samuel Dinsmoor was born at Windham, New Hampshire, in 1766. He walked eight miles each day as a young boy to attend school and then went on to Dartmouth College. To help pay his bills, he taught school and opened a store at Hanover. He graduated from Dartmouth at age nineteen, studied law and opened a practice at Keene in 1792.

Dinsmoor served as postmaster at Keene, organized the Keene Light Infantry and was elected to Congress in 1811. He later served as a state councilor and was elected governor in 1831. It was during his administration that President Andrew Jackson and Vice President Martin Van Buren visited New Hampshire. Dinsmoor was elected to three successive terms as governor. It was he who first recommended to the legislature the formation of a state asylum for the insane. After completing his third term as governor, Dinsmoor returned home to Keene, where he was made first president of the Ashuelot Bank, an office he held until his death.

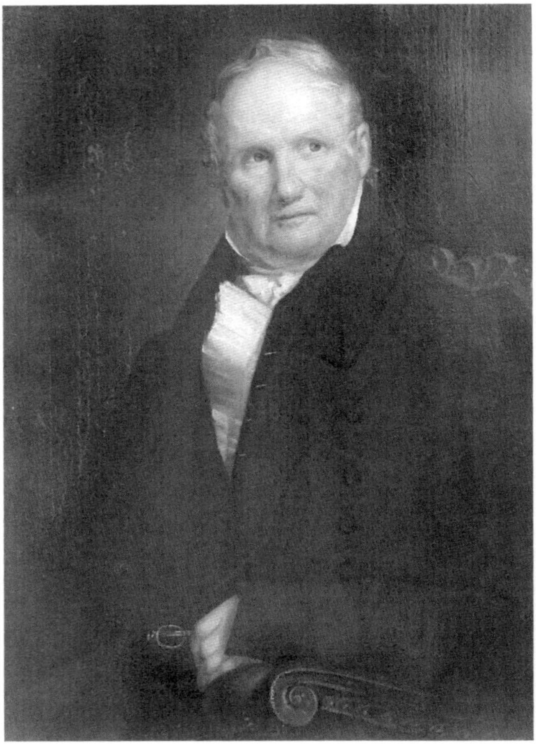

The "Elder Governor" Samuel Dinsmoor.

Samuel Dinsmoor's son, Samuel, was born in Keene in 1799. His life took a course amazingly similar to that of his father. He entered Dartmouth at age eleven and graduated at age fifteen. He then studied law and was admitted to the bar at age nineteen. The younger Samuel was elected clerk of the state senate in 1826 and served several terms in that position. Having learned French at a young age, he was appointed as one of the two commissioners to accompany General Lafayette during his visit to New Hampshire. Dinsmoor was elected governor of the state in 1849, eighteen years after his father was first elected. He also served three terms as the state's chief executive and succeeded his father as president of the Ashuelot Bank.

Samuel Dinsmoor Sr. and Samuel Jr., both Dartmouth graduates, Keene lawyers and presidents of the Ashuelot Bank, are remembered today as the popular, honorable and distinguished governors Samuel Dinsmoor "the elder" and Samuel Dinsmoor "the younger."

THE LOST PRESIDENT

During October 1912, there was a rare presidential visit to Cheshire County: President William Howard Taft toured the region from his summer home in Beverly, Massachusetts.

Following a speech to a large crowd in Newport, Taft started south toward Cheshire County. The president's party consisted of three automobiles, one each for the president, the Secret Service and a group of reporters. The party was led by district highway chief Clarence Brooks. Along the way, Taft was stopped by a group of ladies from the Sunapee Mountain Grange to sign their register and receive honorary membership in the Grange. The president was scheduled to make a brief stop in Marlow, so group leader Brooks went on ahead to organize the crowd there. The party soon followed along behind, but the Secret Service car got a flat tire before they got to Marlow. The car blocked the road so that the other cars could not get around. In an attempt to remain on schedule, the president's car continued on alone down a side road that they hoped was a shortcut to the village.

The Secret Service car and the reporters continued on to Marlow after the tire was changed. The crowd was waiting when they arrived, but President Taft was nowhere to be found. It was now late afternoon, and there was some concern as to his location. The townspeople, reporters and Secret Service organized a search party and started north in search of the president. The side road that Taft had followed was the road to South Acworth, which took him miles out of his way. He eventually turned back the way he had come and was met by the search party. President Taft finally arrived in Marlow, more than two hours late, and was greeted by a crowd of two hundred residents. The president spoke briefly from his automobile and did the same for one hundred well-wishers in Gilsum.

Eight thousand people had gathered in Keene's Central Square by the time the president finally arrived in the city at ten minutes before seven o'clock. The crowd cheered long and loud upon his arrival. Taft was met by Mayor Charles G. Shedd and escorted into the Cheshire House hotel. The president soon appeared on the second-floor balcony of the hotel and gave a brief speech to the eight thousand people below.

He soon traveled on to Marlborough and then to Dublin, where he stayed the night and gave a speech the next morning. President Taft's 1912 visit was the first visit to Keene by a U.S. president during his term of office. Many local residents who saw him that day surely told their grandchildren the story of the day they searched the back roads of Marlow for the president of the United States.

Chesterfield's Chief Justice

Harlan Fiske Stone was born in a small farmhouse on Horseshoe Road in Chesterfield in October 1872. He was the fifth generation of the Stone family to live in the town. The family moved to Amherst, Massachusetts, in 1874, where young Harlan attended Amherst College. He often spent his summer vacations in Chesterfield, where he met Miss Agnes Harvey. The young couple was married at the Harvey home in 1899.

Stone attended Columbia Law School and then became a teacher at the school. In 1910, he was named dean of the law school. Stone gained prominence in the legal profession and in 1924 was named attorney general of the United States. One year later, President Calvin Coolidge appointed him to the Supreme Court.

Stone supported President Roosevelt's New Deal policies and was viewed as a liberal on the court. In October 1941, the month of his sixty-ninth birthday, Roosevelt named Stone chief justice of the United States. Four years later, it was Stone who swore in Harry Truman as president upon the death of Roosevelt. One year later, Stone himself passed away at the age of seventy-three, having served on the Supreme Court for twenty-one years.

The people of Chesterfield never forgot their famous son. In August 1948, they held a memorial service and unveiled a monument at Stone's birthplace on Horseshoe Road. Many national leaders attended the ceremonies. On the same day, a new U.S. postage stamp was issued in honor of Chesterfield's Chief Justice Harlan Fiske Stone.

STEPHEN BULLOCK'S LEGACY

Every four years, New Hampshire experiences another session in the national spotlight in the form of its acclaimed first-in-the-nation presidential primary. Did you know that it was a Cheshire County politician who introduced the piece of legislation from which the primary evolved?

Richmond farmer, fire warden, tax collector and five-term state representative Stephen A. Bullock introduced House Bill 430 in the New Hampshire legislature in 1913. The bill provided for the state's first presidential primary to be held in May 1916. Bullock wished to give all residents a voice in selecting party leaders. His bill was entitled "An Act to provide for the Election of Delegates to National Conventions by Direct Vote of the People." The bill was passed in May 1913, thereby creating the first New Hampshire presidential primary.

The new law was soon amended to move the primary date from May back to March to coincide with the town meeting date. This move was a practical one intended to save towns money by holding one election instead of two. This earlier date resulted in New Hampshire's primary being the earliest held in the nation.

Bullock's law has been further altered over the years. The most important change occurred with the 1952 election when the candidates' names were added to the ballot in addition to the names of convention delegates, thereby allowing citizens to vote directly for the candidate of their choice, resulting in the primary system that we know today. It all began with Richmond's Stephen Bullock, the "grandfather" of New Hampshire's famed first-in-the-nation presidential primary.

Crime, Mystery and Murder

Crime and Punishment in Cheshire County

Early Cheshire County court records illustrate that the punishment for criminal offenses was much different in the county two hundred years ago than it is today. Selling convicted criminals into servitude, branding and public whipping were accepted punishments. In the later part of the eighteenth century, Keene had a public whipping post and a pillory, a wooden device with holes for the head and hands, in which criminals were locked and exposed to public scorn. In the late 1780s, for example, Jacob Putnam of Alstead was convicted of passing counterfeit money and sentenced to stand in the pillory one hour and pay a twenty-five-pound fine and court costs.

Nearly two decades later, in September 1806, Nathan Eldridge was found guilty of burglarizing a store in Walpole and was sentenced to receive nineteen lashes and to be sold into servitude if he could not pay the store owners $1,500 as well as a $500 fine to the county.

The sentence of mutilation was not as common but was indeed used in Cheshire County. In May 1785, Kimball Carleton of Chesterfield was found guilty of forgery and fraud and was sentenced to stand for one hour in the pillory, to have one ear cut off and to pay a fine of $300. Ears were commonly removed in open court by the sheriff, who cut off the ear and then seared the wound with a hot iron.

This public humiliation form of punishment of the olden days was less humane than that used today but may have been an effective deterrent to crime.

FALSE DOLLARS

One of the most notorious counterfeiters in colonial New England was Joshua Howe of Westmoreland, New Hampshire. He was probably the Joshua born in Grafton, Massachusetts, in 1738 and whose family moved to Westmoreland one or two years later.

Howe was arrested at Boston in October 1761 and charged with forging treasurer's notes. He was convicted of counterfeiting and of having tools for making Spanish dollars. He was sentenced to stand for an hour in the pillory, to be given twenty lashes and to pay a fine of ten pounds. He was soon convicted on two additional counterfeiting charges, for which he was fined two hundred pounds, received seventy-eight lashes at the whipping post and was sentenced to two years in prison. A broadside depicting the whipping was printed and distributed at Boston. He was also convicted on a fourth charge of making Spanish dollars and was sentenced to twenty years of hard labor.

Howe was confined to the Springfield, Massachusetts jail for a time but soon managed to return to Westmoreland. A few years later, he was at it once again. Howe paid a debt to Isaac Colton, the former jailer at Springfield, by deeding him a piece of land that he did not own. Colton tracked Howe to Westmoreland, where he was living in a small house with his wife and two children. The former jailer saw counterfeit coins while at Howe's house. Furthermore, Howe bragged that he could make dollars that were only one quarter silver, had a press near his house, was earning money by training other counterfeiters and that he was renting out his counterfeiting tools for ten dollars a day. He was arrested early in 1768 but amazingly was acquitted of all charges.

He returned to Westmoreland but was in jail again the following year for nonpayment of debt. Notorious counterfeiter Joshua Howe later moved to Vermont, where he passed away in 1800.

ROBBERY IN THE DARK VALLEY

Road construction has widened a portion of Route 12 between Keene and Troy that old-timers remember as a dark and forbidding pass between tall ledges and steep hills. It was on this lonely stretch of highway that George Ryan, armed with a knife and pistol, attempted his hand at highway robbery one night in the early 1800s.

Young Ryan, a resident of Canada, had been travelling through the states on horseback. He stopped off at Keene for a few days, drinking and gambling, and spent the last of his money. As a result, he went out to the narrow valley to replenish his purse.

The first man he met was a poor teamster in his sleigh. The teamster surrendered all of his money, four cents, and Ryan escaped into the woods. The teamster went for help and came back after the robber. Ryan left his horse and fled into the forest. A search was organized along the roadside, and Ryan was soon driven onto the highway, where he was confronted by a young physician who was posted there to watch for him. Ryan drew his gun and aimed it at the chest of the young man. The gun misfired, however, and Ryan drew his knife. The weapon had a delicate blade and was rendered useless in the ensuing struggle. The young physician cried for help, and Ryan the robber was finally captured.

Ryan was soon brought to trial, and although he was not sent to jail for his crimes, the story of highway robbery in the dark valley became a legend along the road to Troy.

Acworth Grave Robbing

Back in 1824, the Old Cemetery in the town of Acworth was the scene of a late-night grave robbing. Despite its terrible nature, the crime of grave robbing was apparently not unusual at that time as a means of obtaining cadavers for the purpose of laboratory study and dissection.

On October 31, 1824, forty-three-year-old Bezaleel Beckwith passed away and was buried in the Acworth Cemetery. Thirteen days later, it was discovered that his body had been stolen from the grave. Suspicion was immediately placed on medical students from Dartmouth, who had gained a reputation as body snatchers. Shortly thereafter, however, James Wilson Jr. of Acworth was arrested at Castleton, Vermont, and charged with stealing the body for the purpose of dissection. Wilson was returned to Acworth, where he was held for trial. Bail was set at $700, but the case never went to trial and the bail was forfeited. Wilson's arrest at Castleton would seem to indicate that Beckwith's body might have been stolen for dissection at the Castleton Medical Academy, but local residents still felt that Dartmouth boys were involved in the crime.

Beckwith's friends erected a stone over his grave with the following verse:

This stone tells of the death of Bezaleel Beckwith, not where his body lies. He died Oct. 31, 1824 age 43. The thirteenth day after his body was stolen from the grave.

Now twice bereaved the mourner cries
My friend is dead, his body gone,
God's act is just my heart replies,
Forgive, oh God, what man has done.

THE HAUNTED BARN OF TROY

Considerable excitement was aroused in the town of Troy, New Hampshire, in the winter of 1818 when what appeared to be human bones were discovered on the site of a barn that burned down in the town. The fire exposed what looked like a burial mound below where the floor of the barn had been. Upon investigation, bones were found on the site.

Rumors of murder began to circulate, and the selectmen ran an advertisement in the *New Hampshire Sentinel* asking for information that would help to solve the mystery. Several months later, Joseph Nimblet of Woodstock, Vermont, appeared in Troy and revealed that fourteen years earlier his brother-in-law had disappeared on a trip from Provincetown, Massachusetts, to Woodstock, Vermont. Brother-in-law Lucas had been carrying a large sum of money and was last seen at the Harris Tavern in Troy.

Residents of Troy had suspected for years that dark deeds had taken place at the barn. Leading citizens claimed to have seen strange lights and heard unusual noises near the building. Many local people avoided the area whenever possible. They now began to see some substance to their suspicions.

Some local residents believed that the man who had disappeared had left the tavern with two local residents to visit a farm that one of the men hoped to sell to him. That farm was the very place where the bones were found.

Public opinion was very strong and the two men were arrested. Neither of them was convicted in connection with the case, and the mystery of Troy's haunted barn was never solved.

Murder at the Bowling Alley

More than 150 years ago, a bowling alley was built east of Keene's Main Street near where the Beaver Mills buildings now stand. The alley was a popular place and patronized by many leading citizens. During the mid-1850s, however, the reputation of the alley took a bad turn. It became a vile place with many disreputable characters visiting the alley's barroom and the three ladies who operated the business.

On November 22, 1864, the community was startled by a report that a murder had occurred at the alley. Miss Sarah Webber, one of the three ladies who lived there, had taken a pistol from behind the bar and shot Alfred Tolman in the head. He died the next morning. Sarah Webber surrendered to the police and was placed in jail. She pleaded not guilty to a charge of murder.

Miss Webber's trial took place in April 1865. The case caused considerable excitement in the community. The indictment charged that her act was premeditated. Her lawyers claimed that she had acted in self-defense and that, in fact, Alfred Tolman had attacked Miss Webber just before she shot him. After a five-day trial, the jury brought in a verdict of manslaughter. Miss Webber was sentenced to one day of solitary confinement and fifteen years of hard labor in the state prison.

Her lawyers finally found two witnesses to the shooting who admitted that she had shot Tolman in self-defense. Governor Weston pardoned Miss Webber in 1871. At about the same time, the bowling alley was removed forever from Keene's east side.

The Murder of Alvin Foster

On the morning of May 24, 1876, the citizens of Keene were startled to learn that businessman Alvin Foster had been found murdered in front of the Washington Street School. He was found lying on his face with a sponge saturated with chloroform under his nose. There were no other signs of violence on his body.

Foster, who was highly respected in Keene, left a wife and child. The coroner determined that he had died of suffocation by chloroform, and a police investigation was begun. Although a Vermont man was arrested, he was soon released, and little progress was made in the case for several months.

A year and a half after Foster's death, George Hamilton was arrested for the murder in Louisiana and sent to Keene to stand trial. Hamilton had lived in Keene for a while and had made some suspicious remarks about the case to people in the South. It was soon determined, however, that Hamilton had contrived the entire situation and used the arrest as a means of escaping from Louisiana, where he was suspected of another murder. After another year and a half, Frederick Dodge of Vermont was arrested for the murder. The investigation had shown that Foster and Dodge had been rivals for the affection of a young widow who had moved to Keene shortly before Foster's death and whom he had visited often at her hotel room. It was suggested that Foster had been the victim of a lover's triangle, but Dodge gave evidence that he was elsewhere on the night of the murder and was acquitted of the charges. Many local residents felt that Foster had committed suicide, but the circumstances of the death were never proven and the case of Alvin Foster was never solved.

Frail Jail

Keene's original log jail was replaced in 1785 when a new wood-frame structure was built on what became known as Prison Street, now Washington Street. A whipping post was erected in the front yard.

It was not long before the jail became a local joke because of frequent breaks. The first escape occurred just five years after the jail was built. Thomas Brintnall and Berry Chase escaped on the night of January 22, 1790. For more than a month, Haneniah Hall, the jailer, offered a forty-dollar reward in the local newspaper for their return. Hall described Brintnall as about forty years of age; light in complexion; five feet, nine inches high; wearing a blue coat; and recently a resident of Westmoreland. Chase was described as forty-five years old; dark in complexion; five feet, ten inches tall; a resident of Swanzey; very talkative; and much addicted to new-light preaching. Hall offered twenty dollars for the return of either of these men to the jail. The advertisements disappeared after a month, but the newspaper did not report that the men were recaptured.

A convict by the name of Hicks once escaped by smearing himself with soap and slipping out of a window. Mr. Loveland, perhaps having heard of other jail breaks, also tried to escape through a window. One rainy night he

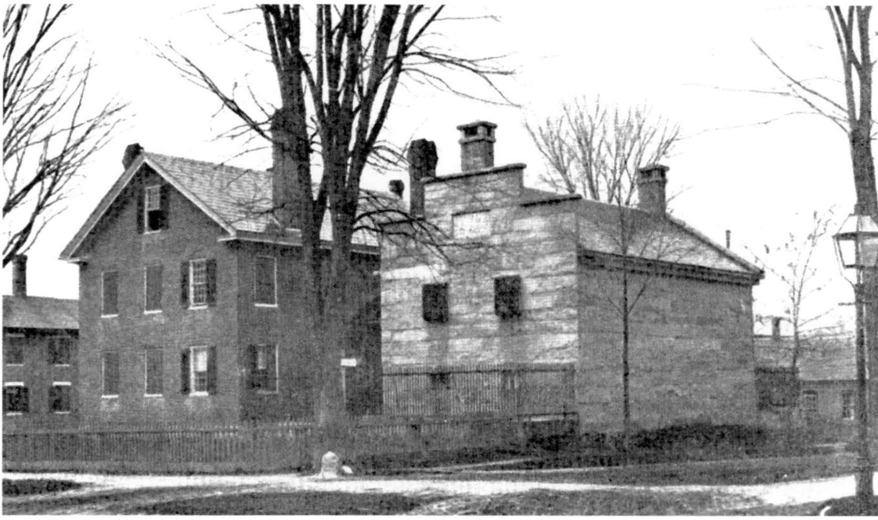

The jailer's house and the "new" Keene jail, built in 1833.

took off his clothes, hung them on a nail outside the window and then tried to climb out. He was a large man and became stuck in the window frame. After struggling for some time, he yelled for help. It was necessary to remove the whole window frame to release him.

Several people confined for debt all escaped together one evening. They visited the glass factory to watch the blowing for a while, got a drink at a local store and then returned to the jail. They woke the jailer to let them in, but he told them to come back in the morning and not to disturb his sleep again.

This situation continued for almost fifty years. The escape of three more prisoners in 1830 proved to be the final straw. The old wooden structure was replaced with a new jail in 1833. This one was much more secure; the new two-story jail contained seven cells and was constructed with 1,400 tons of Roxbury granite.

The Bungling Bank Robbers

At about nine o'clock on the evening of June 11, 1850, Abijah Larned and an accomplice broke into the bank at Charlestown, New Hampshire. By midnight they had loaded nearly $12,000 in gold, silver and bills into their carriage and drove peacefully out of town.

Eleven miles to the south they came to the long hill between Drewsville and Marlow. They decided to get out of the carriage so that their horse would have less weight to carry up the hill. One man walked in front of the carriage and one man behind. When they arrived at the top of the hill, the horse and carriage were nowhere to be seen. Each man thought that the other had been guiding the horse. They went back down the hill but still could not find the carriage. They searched for a few hours in the dark but, realizing that the authorities would soon be searching for them, made their escape as morning arrived. At about the same hour, Horace Gee of Marlow found the horse and carriage wandering in the road near his home. Mr. Gee soon learned of the robbery and returned the money to Charlestown to claim a reward that had been offered.

Abijah Larned was later arrested and agreed to return to Charlestown to stand trial, probably in part so that he could learn what had happened to his carriage of riches. He asked to be taken before the bank officers, before whom he confessed to the crime and apologized for the trouble he had caused. Furthermore, he insisted that he repay any expenses incurred by the crime, including damage done to the vault and the reward paid to Horace Gee. Larned told the story of the lost carriage, and it was determined that the horse had turned off on a side road halfway up the long hill and peacefully continued along to Gee's house in Marlow.

Larned's apology so impressed the local officials that they returned his burglar's tools and allowed him to leave Charlestown after posting a small bail. Needless to say, Larned jumped bail and never returned to stand trial. He did continue to use his burglar's tools, however, and was later arrested and jailed for robbing the bank at Cooperstown, New York.

GENTLEMAN BANK ROBBER

German native Mark Shinborn came to the United States in 1860. This well-educated and well-mannered young man earned money as a gambler and purchased a fine farm and mansion near Saratoga, New York. Making use of what he learned at a temporary job at a safe company, he robbed the bank at Walpole of $40,000 in November 1864. He was arrested six months later and returned to Keene for trial. Shinborn attracted a great deal of attention in Keene, especially from the young ladies of the town. He was sentenced to ten years at the state prison but escaped from the Keene jail with the help of a friend. He escaped into the woods despite being closely pursued by a group of residents. He was recaptured several months later and sent to the state prison at Concord. He escaped from jail once again late in 1866 and returned to Keene.

Shinborn lived unrecognized at the Cheshire House for several weeks planning a robbery at the Ashuelot Bank. He entered the home of the cashier, made impressions of the keys and had a duplicate set made. When he got to the bank, however, he found only $1,000 in the vault. This was not enough, and he waited for more money to be deposited. He soon entered the bank again, but now there was too much money to carry. He went to New York to get help with the job but never returned.

In New York, Shinborn robbed a bank of about $1 million and escaped to live in Europe. He bought a title, lost his fortune, took to robbery again and was arrested and sent to prison for fourteen years. He soon secured a pardon, however, and returned to the United States to continue his craft. He was arrested in 1895 and sent to prison for five years. When he was released, at age sixty-eight, he was arrested again for the Walpole robbery. He was sent to prison at Concord to serve out his term, during which time he told anyone who would listen that he was *not* Mark Shinborn.

Joe Haywood Meets Jesse James

Joseph L. Haywood, a native of Fitzwilliam, New Hampshire, has a sad and unusual claim to fame. It has to do with his meeting with the famous outlaw Jesse James during the 1870s.

Joseph, the son of Benjamin Haywood, was born in Fitzwilliam in 1837. He lived in the town until he went west to seek his fortune at age twenty-three. He worked for two years in Michigan and Illinois before enlisting to fight in the Civil War in 1862. He served throughout the war and then moved to Minnesota, where he lived and worked as a bookkeeper in the town of Northfield.

By 1872, Haywood was bookkeeper for the First National Bank of Northfield. In September of that year, the cashier was away from the bank, and Haywood was in charge as acting cashier. On September 7, he was working in the bank with the teller and assistant bookkeeper when a band of eight mounted bank robbers entered the town. It was the famous Jesse James gang. Three members of the gang entered the bank while the other five stayed on the street to intimidate anyone who might try to come to the rescue. Haywood refused to hand over the money, however, and the citizens quickly came to help. Two of the robbers were killed, and the gang was forced to leave the bank without any cash. As the last robber was leaving the bank, reported by Fitzwilliam residents to have been Jesse James himself, he turned and fired a fatal shot at Haywood. The sad claim to fame of Fitzwilliam's Joe Haywood is that he died in the famous Northfield raid at the hands of outlaw Jesse James.

LANGDON MOORE, SAFECRACKER

Langdon Moore was born in East Washington, New Hampshire, in 1830. His parents were farmers, and Moore spent his entire boyhood on farms. At age twenty-three, the country boy visited a gambling house in Boston. Although he lost money there, he decided that gambling was a good field to learn more about. Moore took an alias, moved to New York and became a card dealer at a gambling club. By age twenty-six, he was part owner of his own gambling saloon.

During that year, he visited Massachusetts, passed two hundred counterfeit ten-dollar bills at an Athol bank and was promptly arrested. Moore's father bailed him out. Rather than reforming, however, Moore decided to improve his method of counterfeiting. When the Secret Service began to close in, he moved to Natick, Massachusetts, and began to study and sell safes and vaults.

With the knowledge gained from this new undertaking, Moore and an accomplice cleaned out the vault of the Concord, Massachusetts National Bank when the cashier was out to lunch one afternoon in September 1865. They walked out with a feed bag containing $310,000, none of which was ever recovered by the authorities. This began a string of some one hundred robberies undertaken by Moore over the next fifteen years. He was finally arrested and convicted for some of his crimes and spent several years in both the Maine and Massachusetts state prisons.

Moore was old and tired when released from prison. He found comfort with his old friend, playwright Denman Thompson of Swanzey. Thompson built

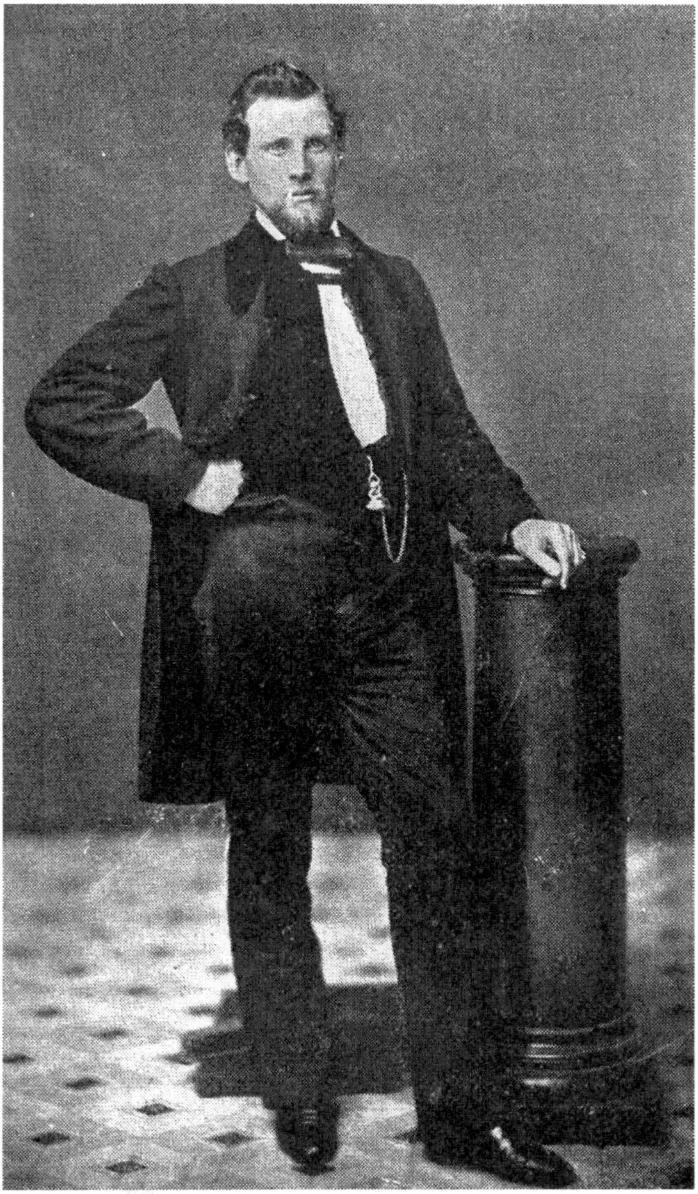

Langdon Moore.

him a cottage on the shores of Swanzey Lake. Moore spent his final days there and was remembered by a local resident as "always neat, kind and sociable." Bank robber Langdon Moore published a 650-page autobiography of his eventful life in 1893 and passed away in Swanzey at age eighty in 1910.

Fires, Disasters and Destructive Weather

The Dark Day

May 19 marks the anniversary of a day on which the sun disappeared and many of our ancestors felt that Judgment Day was at hand. On Friday, May 19, 1780, the sun was obscured by a strange darkness ranging from New Jersey and New York across Connecticut, Rhode Island, Massachusetts, southern New Hampshire and into Maine.

In mid-morning of that day, Cheshire County residents noticed a large dark cloud to the west. The cloud soon covered the whole sky. It was so dark at noon that the cows came in from the fields and birds went to roost. Elias Hemenway of Marlborough had to stop plowing his fields at noon because there was not enough light for him to work by. Local residents ate their midday meal by candlelight.

Local diarists Abner Sanger of Keene and Miriam Newton of Marlborough both recorded the event in their diaries. Mrs. Newton mentioned using candles at midday, but both writers seemed to take the dark day in stride. Many did not take it so lightly, however. Superstitious people across New England feared the worst and took the darkness as a terrifying sign from heaven. It was later determined that the fearful darkness was probably caused by the smoke of huge forest fires in western New England and New York. Despite the logical explanations, the Dark Day of May 1780 was remembered and discussed with awe by a generation of New Englanders.

THE YEAR WITHOUT A SUMMER

Although there are many complaints about the lack of summer in some years, our ancestors experienced a summer unknown to current generations. The severe weather during the year of 1816 has become known as "the year without a summer."

The spring season that year was cold, with the ground frozen solid on May 15. Warm weather arrived with the month of June as temperatures rose into the eighties. On June 5, however, Keene was hit with a heavy frost, and the ground froze every night for the next week. Snow fell in the region on June 6, 7 and 11. Vegetable gardens were destroyed and had to be replanted. Corn and hay crops were endangered.

July brought little relief. Frost was reported four days in succession during the first week of July and again on the ninth and seventeenth. In addition to the cold, the region experienced a drought from the end of June to the end of September. Some people to the north were forced to sell their livestock because there was not enough hay for feed.

August 21 and 28 saw more frost descend on Keene, ending all hope for the corn crop. The corn in the fields was cut up for animal feed, and the entire crop failed in Swanzey, where the town subsisted on emergency supplies from other towns.

The summer ended with several more nights of frost in September. Hay was almost nonexistent, and trees were felled so that the livestock could feed on the leaves and branches. Many cattle died before the winter passed. Food and hay prices increased dramatically, and passenger pigeons supplemented the sparse diets. Although 1817 brought a normal summer season, our ancestors never forgot "the year without a summer."

THE GRASSHOPPER YEAR

The spring of 1826 began on an ominous note. The *New Hampshire Sentinel* reported that on only one morning in March was the sun visible through the clouds. The weather then improved a bit until May, when the temperature rose into the nineties day after day and very little rain fell. Even less rain fell during the month of June.

The fields of Cheshire County turned brown as the drought took hold. It was then that the grasshoppers arrived. Huge clouds of the insects filled the sky in and around Keene. They rose in the air by the thousands before every step of the traveler. The farmers had feared that the drought would destroy the crops, but now the grasshoppers devastated all vegetation. One man attempted to save his garden by picking the insects off his plants. He took his baskets out to the garden one morning and picked nearly six bushels of the creatures before breakfast. At dusk, the fences in Swanzey were covered by the grasshoppers as they settled down for the night. It was reported that after the vegetation was gone, the insects began to eat recently produced hoe handles.

Rain finally came during the month of July. Once the rain started, however, it did not stop. The grasshoppers were washed away, along with nearly every bridge in the town of Swanzey. September was a perfect growing month, and our ancestors survived the drought, floods and insects, but for many years thereafter the residents of the region referred to 1826 as "the Grasshopper Year."

The Tornado of 1877

Late afternoon activities on Sunday, July 1, 1877, were interrupted by a violent storm that cut a swath through Gilsum, Sullivan, Nelson and Hancock. The storm was preceded by a black cloud and heavy rain that came eastward over Surry Mountain. Suddenly, a strong wind struck the Webster barn in Gilsum, destroying it in a matter of moments. The winds then drove to the southeast, destroying nine barns, two sugar houses, three apple orchards and the home of William Wilder and seriously damaged two other homes before moving on to Sullivan. The whirlwind also picked up the District 3 schoolhouse in Gilsum, turned it one quarter around and placed it back on the foundation without damaging the plaster on the walls.

In Sullivan, the storm destroyed two barns and moved two houses from their foundations. Ten-year-old F.R. Bond was carried some one hundred feet through the air by the wind and then landed safely on the ground. Edwin Blood was leading his horse and carriage to the barn when the wind struck. He was lifted up into the air and landed back on his feet unhurt, but then he saw his carriage flying toward him over his horse's back. He ran to his house, where he found that the roof was gone.

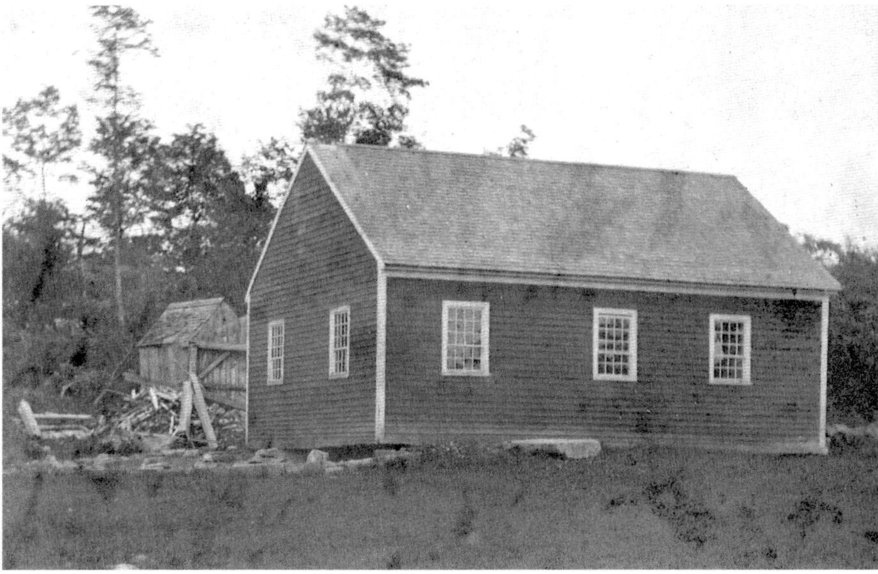

The District #3 schoolhouse in Gilsum, after it was lifted and turned around by the tornado of 1877.

The whirlwind came and went within two minutes. It passed through East Sullivan village, on into Nelson and blew itself out in Hancock. One thousand people came to Gilsum and Sullivan the next day to view the damage. The tornado of 1877 was remembered by local residents as the "most sensational freak of nature ever experienced" in their town.

The Blizzard of '88

In March 1888, a three-day blizzard buried the Northeast, and it remains the storm with which New England blizzards are still compared today.

The snowstorm paralyzed Atlantic coast cities north of Virginia before it arrived in New Hampshire on Sunday evening, March 11. By mid-morning on Monday, travel was nearly impossible in the region. The heavy snowfall combined with gale-force winds to create snowdrifts as tall as twelve to fifteen feet high. All roads in Keene and throughout the county were soon impassable.

The telegraph lines were soon knocked down, and all trains were stranded in the snow. Stagecoaches were unable to travel, and the mail was delayed

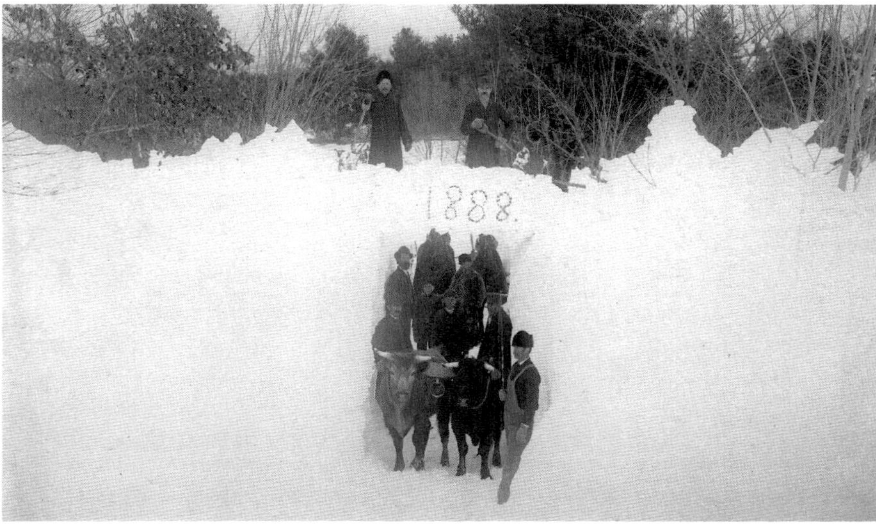

Clearing the roads in Swanzey after the Blizzard of 1888.

for several days. Businesses were closed, and town meetings were postponed on Tuesday because no one could get to the town halls.

When the storm finally let up on Wednesday the fourteenth, Keene had thirty-six inches of snow, Chesterfield forty inches and Dublin forty-two. These accumulations combined with the high winds resulted in many houses being buried to roof level. The blizzard resulted in some four hundred deaths and $20 million in damages throughout the Northeast. It was several days before the roads were cleared, the trains and mails began to move again and the region returned to normal. Keene's *Cheshire Republican* may have summed up the impact of the storm best when it reported that "the storm of this week is the most severe of any known to have visited this section of the country."

The Hurricane of 1938

In mid-September 1938, a strong hurricane worked its way up the Atlantic coast. The storm did not veer off over the ocean, however, as is typical for such storms. Taking the path of least resistance, the storm rushed northward into an area of low pressure in the Connecticut River Valley.

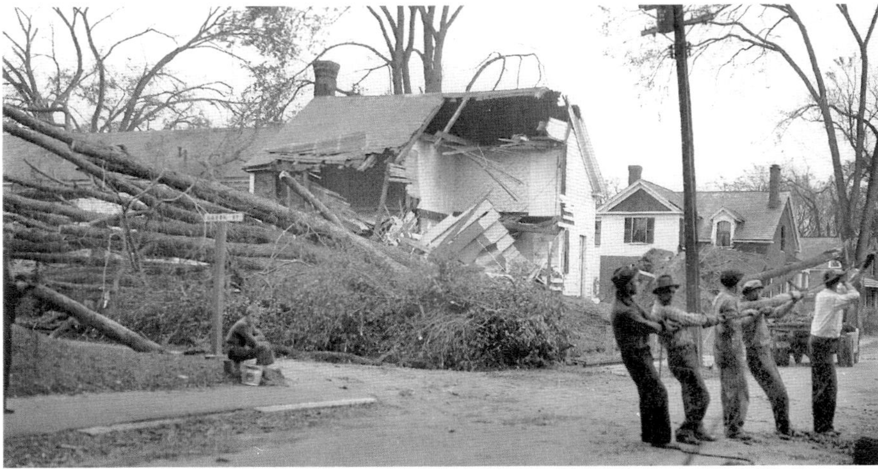

Above: Hurricane damage and cleanup on Keene's Union Street after the Hurricane of 1938.

Below: Damage to the Sargent Motor Company on Mechanic Street in Keene caused by the Hurricane of 1938.

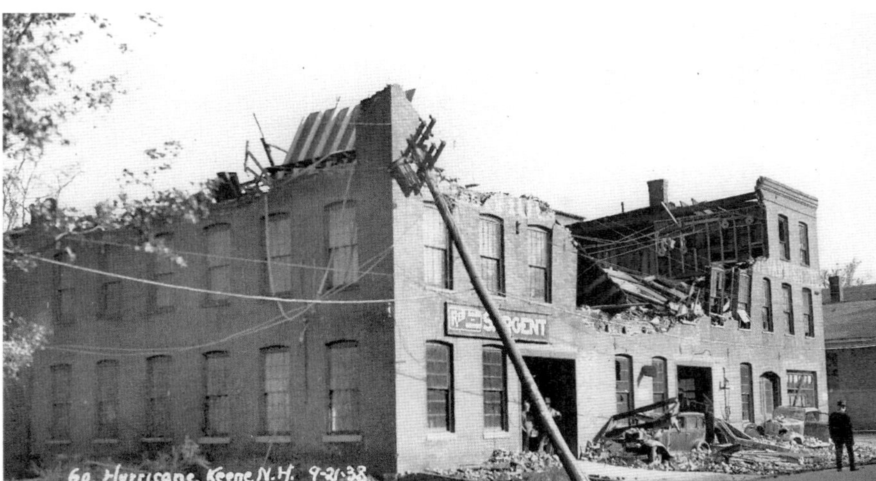

At about 5:00 p.m. on Wednesday, September 21, the hurricane struck Cheshire County. Suddenly, a southeast wind hit the region with frightening strength, toppling trees and chimneys. The wind continued unabated for an hour and a half and decreased very little until after midnight. One woman in Nelson could not close the doors of her house against the wind. She sat cowering in the dark for hours as the wind rushed through her home. Local residents sat in fear throughout the night as trees snapped and small buildings flew through the air.

Thursday morning was bright and sunny, but the combined damage of the wind and more than six inches of rain was unbelievable. The streets of Keene were flooded or jammed with fallen trees. Travel was impossible and all lines of communication were severed. Two thousand shade trees had toppled, and the forests in the city's parks were blown flat. Several homes and businesses received extensive damage. Cars were crushed, steeples toppled and roofs blown off, and three hundred people evacuated from their homes. Hundreds of workers struggled for days to clear the streets and repair the telephone and electric lines. Keene suffered $1 million in damages. The scene was the same throughout the county. Despite the unbelievable damage, not one local resident was seriously injured by the famous Hurricane of 1938.

The Great Fire of Keene

The most devastating fire in Keene's history occurred in 1865. Shortly before midnight on October 14 of that year, a guest at the Cheshire House hotel discovered a fire in the basement of Knowlton's Hardware store in Richards Block on the corner of Roxbury Street and Central Square. The fire department, consisting of two pumpers, a hose reel and a hook and ladder, responded immediately, but it soon became evident that the block was lost.

A strong breeze fanned the flames, and the crews turned their attention to other buildings nearby. They went to work on the Cheshire House to the south and other buildings to the east that caught on fire several times. Landlord Doolittle of the Cheshire House organized a crew of guests and employees to help save the hotel. Just as the firemen began to get the flames under control, the water in the reservoir at the head of Main Street ran out. A pumper was sent to Beaver Brook, and it pumped water to the fire, but it was too little, too late.

The blocks to the north could not be saved. The firemen turned their attention to city hall and managed to save it, but three hours after the alarm was sounded, the entire east side of Central Square was a smoking ruin. Damages amounted to $70,000, less than half of which was covered by insurance. Five years passed before that side of the square was rebuilt.

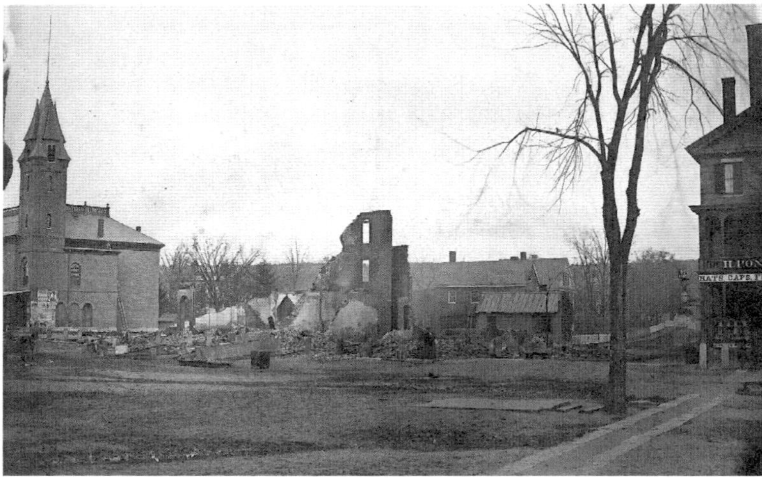

The east side of Central Square the morning after the devastating fire of 1865.

The installation of a water system downtown had been discussed for several years, but it was controversial and there was considerable opposition. The lack of water to fight the great fire of 1865 settled the issue, however. Keene's first water system was installed from Goose Pond to Central Square in 1869.

The Marlow-Stoddard Forest Fire

As we look back now, two generations later, it seems almost inevitable that New Hampshire's worst forest fire ever would occur in April 1941. During that month the state had experienced the highest average temperature and lowest average rainfall of any single month in seventy years. The forests were clogged with blown-down timber as a result of the 1938 hurricane. Numerous crews had set up sawmills to remove the timber.

It was at one of these sawmills in the northern section of Marlow that the fire was accidentally ignited on the afternoon of April 28. The fire quickly raced southward, burning the full length of Marlow and into the town of Gilsum. The next day the wind shifted, and the fire spread rapidly toward Marlow village. Ten local fire departments worked to save the village as the fire raced through dry fields and up to the houses themselves. It burned all around the homes, isolating the people of Marlow, but the village was saved.

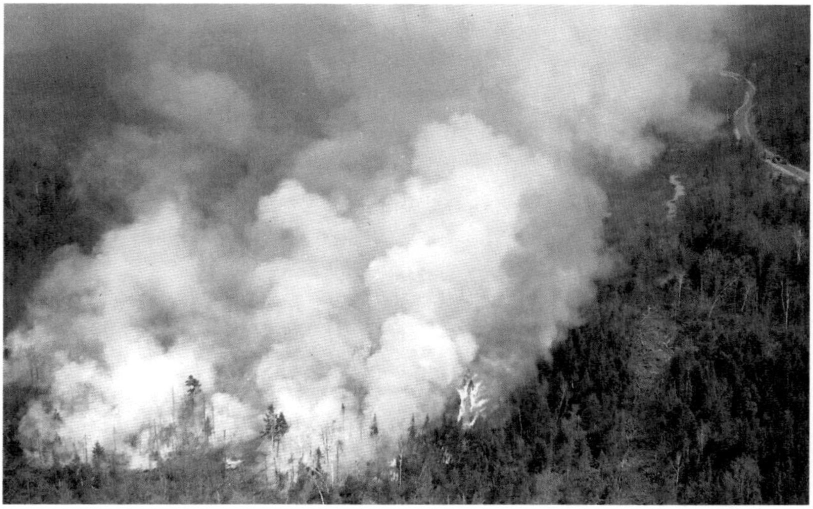

Above: A portion of the Marlow/Stoddard forest fire as seen from the air.

Below: The smoldering remains of a house destroyed by the Marlow/Stoddard forest fire.

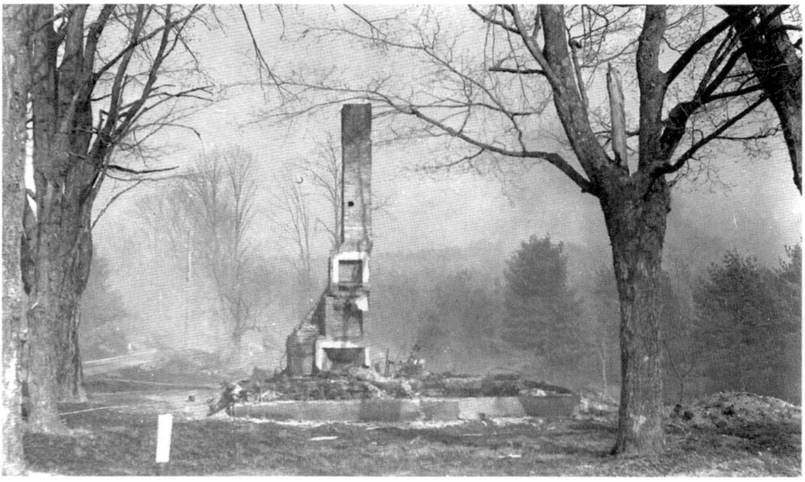

Fred Jennings, the watchman in the lookout tower on Pitcher Mountain in Stoddard, made reports on the fire's progress as it raged into Stoddard. He finally fled down the mountain as the lookout tower burned behind him. The village of Stoddard was saved as rowboats were placed along the road and filled with water as a means of transferring water up the road to the fire. It continued to burn into April 30, but the wind died down and snow and rain began to fall, aiding the crews in finally extinguishing the blaze. In just over two days many homes and twenty-seven thousand acres had burned. Approximately 48 percent of Marlow's land area, 42 percent of Stoddard and smaller portions of Washington and Gilsum had been devastated. Although many were left homeless, not one person was injured in the blaze, including the two thousand men who had converged on the towns to fight the great Marlow-Stoddard forest fire.

War and Warriors

Arnold's Expedition

On November 1, 1775, Ebenezer Tolman of Fitzwilliam, New Hampshire, found himself deep in the frozen wilderness of northern Maine. Seven weeks earlier, he had marched from Cambridge, Massachusetts, with 1,100 other colonial soldiers under the command of Benedict Arnold with orders from General Washington to march north in an attempt to capture Quebec from the British.

On the evening of November 1, Tolman wrote in his journal: "This morning started very early and hungry and little satisfied with our night's rest. Travelled all day very briskly, and at night encamped in a miserable situation. Here we killed a dog and we made a very great feast without either bread or salt, we having been 4 or 5 days without provisions." The surviving troops were in a desperate situation; they were without food, in freezing weather and still seventy miles from inhabited settlements.

Soldier and historian Simon G. Griffin described Arnold's expedition as the "greatest adventure of the whole Revolutionary War." Ebenezer Tolman was one of thirteen Cheshire County men who took part in this legendary march through the wilderness. The purpose of Arnold's expedition was to surprise the British forces at Quebec and capture the city, thereby convincing Canada to join the Revolutionary cause.

Tolman recorded in his journal that his battalion left Cambridge on September 13 and marched to Newburyport, where the troops embarked for Maine aboard eleven little vessels. The small fleet soon entered the mouth of the Kennebec River and landed at the town of Gardiner. The troops waited a few days at Fort Western (now Augusta) while construction was completed on the last of 220 bateaux built for the expedition. On September 25, the men plunged into the wilderness and their terrible struggle began.

The boats had been quickly built from green wood and were very heavy and poorly made. The troops spent more time pulling and carrying the boats than they did riding in them. The men were wet much of the day, and their clothes froze stiff at night. Rain began to fall and continued day after day. Many of the provisions were spoiled, and the ground became a stew of black mud. Then the snow began to fall. Many men became sick and were sent back the way they had come.

Tolman and his comrades continued on with the main column. They abandoned the remaining bateaux on October 27 and continued on foot. By the end of October, their provisions were gone. The men dug roots from the frozen dirt and hoped to find wildlife to eat. More men weakened, became sick and could not continue. There was nothing to be done for them, and about one hundred men were left by the trail in a few days' time.

Robert Worsley of Keene also recalled the meal of dog meat that was recounted by Tolman. The dog emerged from the woods, barked once and was immediately shot. Worsley was assigned the duty of dressing the poor animal. As he began the chore, the starving men snatched away the flesh, leaving him only what he could grasp in his hands.

The soldiers stumbled up and down the hills. They began to eat their leather moccasins and breeches. Tolman wrote that they "staggered about like drunken men." Finally, just as survival seemed impossible, men from the front of the column came back toward them, leading cattle and carrying provisions; they had reached the settlements outside of Quebec.

Only 510 of the 1,100 men who began the march arrived at Quebec. They were emaciated, many almost naked, and they had little ammunition but were determined to continue their mission. Arnold's troops were joined by 250 men under General Montgomery, who had marched north up the Hudson River. The troops laid siege to Quebec, and then, at two o'clock on the morning of December 31, they waded through snowdrifts to attack the city. Quebec had been reinforced with 1,800 British soldiers shortly before the colonial forces arrived, however, and the attack was doomed to failure. More than 200 members of the colonial force were killed or wounded, and 372 were taken prisoner. Tolman and his comrades began seven months of miserable imprisonment. The British exchanged the prisoners in the summer of 1776, believing that their terrible experience had proven to them the true power of England and that the former prisoners would argue for peace throughout the thirteen colonies. In August 1776, Arnold's men were released and shipped to New York.

The British plan failed, however, as Ebenezer Tolman and many of the other former prisoners rejoined the military as soon as possible. Tolman himself reenlisted in the army for three years in 1777 but was unable to complete his term due to ill health. He moved to Nelson, New Hampshire, after the war and died there in 1838 at the age of ninety, more than sixty years after he served in one of the most dramatic military missions in American history.

Reuben Kendall, Soldier

During the year 1818, Reuben Kendall of Richmond submitted a pension claim for Revolutionary War service to the Cheshire County court of common pleas. The claim began as follows: "I, Reuben Kendall, a black man born in Africa, not far from ninety years of age, now of Richmond, in the County of Cheshire and State of New Hampshire, testify and declare: that I served in the War of the Revolution in the Continental establishment."

Kendall's story is an interesting tale of slavery and military service. Kendall was captured in Africa and sold into slavery in Salem, Massachusetts. He was purchased by Ethan Kendall of Lancaster, Massachusetts. The slave, known as Jittem in his native Africa, was given the name Reuben Kendall by his master. During the Revolutionary War, Kendall was offered his freedom if he would serve in the army as a substitute for his master Ethan. Kendall agreed, was given his freedom and enlisted in the Fifteenth Massachusetts Regiment in September 1777. He served throughout the war, a total of nearly seven years. Kendall participated in the Battles of Stillwater, Saratoga and Monmouth and was at Yorktown when Cornwallis surrendered.

Kendall came to Richmond with his family in about 1795. He was granted a pension of eight dollars per month as a result of his 1818 application. Two years later, at the age of ninety, Reuben Kendall passed away. He and his wife were buried in the Quaker burying yard. Their graves were unmarked for more than 160 years until 1981, when a group of Richmond townspeople placed a veteran's grave marker and American flag on the grave of black Revolutionary War veteran Reuben Kendall.

The Oldest Soldier

Samuel Downing was born in Newburyport, Massachusetts, late in the year 1761. When he was nine years of age, Samuel was playing one day with some of his young friends. A stranger came by and asked if any of the boys wanted to go with him to learn how to make spinning wheels. Samuel agreed to go. He said that his parents were away for the day, but that wouldn't matter much. As a result, young Samuel came to Antrim, Hew Hampshire, to make spinning wheel spokes at the mill of Thomas Aiken.

Samuel's parents thought that he had fallen into the ocean and drowned. Samuel became very homesick but could not contact his parents and did not know the way home. Thomas Aiken eventually contacted Samuel's parents, but he stayed on in Antrim making spinning wheels.

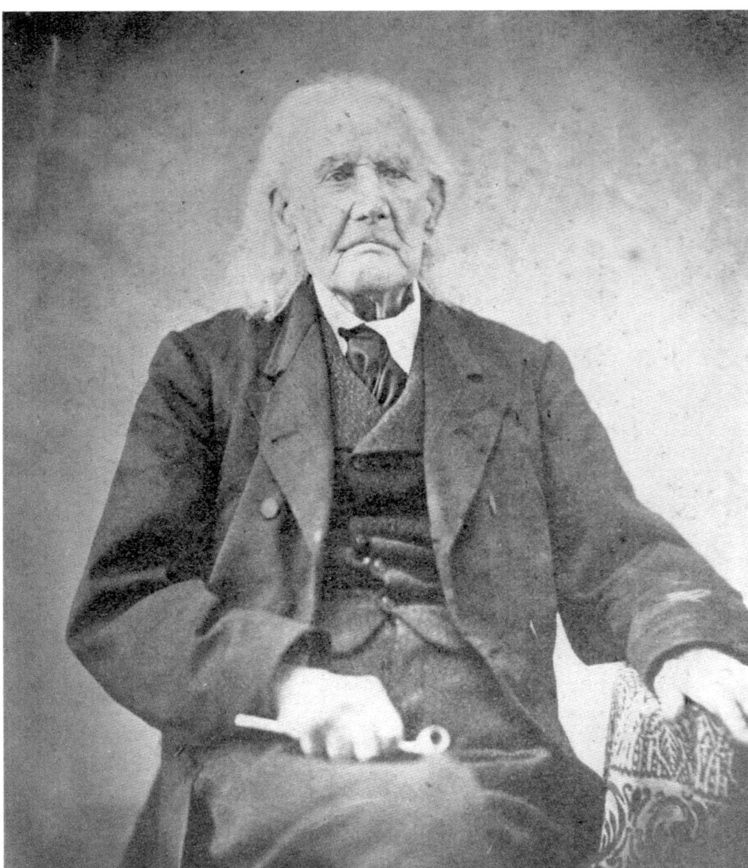

Samuel Downing.

At age fifteen, Samuel ran away from the Aiken home to join the Revolutionary army. He met up with his father, whom he had not seen for several years, and the two fought side by side. Samuel served for four years until the end of the war. He returned to Antrim after the fighting ended and married a local girl. He farmed in Antrim for many years and eventually moved to New York State.

When the Civil War began in 1861, Samuel was a hale and hearty ninety years of age. As a soldier of the Revolution, his views on the Civil War were often quoted. He said that if the rebels came north he would "take up his gun and meet them" and that if "Old General" Washington was alive, he would "hang every rebel to the nearest tree."

When Antrim's Samuel Downing died at the age of 105 in 1867, it was reported that he had been the last surviving veteran of the American Revolutionary War. The same claim was made about three other men who died over the next few years. With the death of these last Revolutionary War veterans, an important chapter in American history was brought to a close.

Amos Pollard at the Alamo

In 1836, the state of Texas won its independence from Mexico. The Alamo is the site of one of the most remembered battles during this struggle for independence. Of the 180 men who fought and died at the Alamo, one of the defenders was a man from Surry, New Hampshire.

Amos Pollard was born in Ashburnham, Massachusetts, in 1803. The Pollard family moved to Surry when Amos was five years old. His father ran a tavern in Surry and Amos grew up in the town.

After completing his education in Surry public schools, Amos Pollard went to New York for medical training. After completing his education, Dr. Pollard traveled to the South and visited Texas in 1834. Leaving a wife and child in New York in 1834, Pollard became active in the Texas independence movement, devoting his time to that cause.

By January 1836, Dr. Pollard was chief surgeon of the force at the Alamo. On February 13, he wrote to Texas governor Henry Smith, telling him that "my department is nearly destitute of medicine and in the event of a siege I can be very little use to the sick under such circumstances…we are threatened with a large invading army…Let us show them how republicans can and

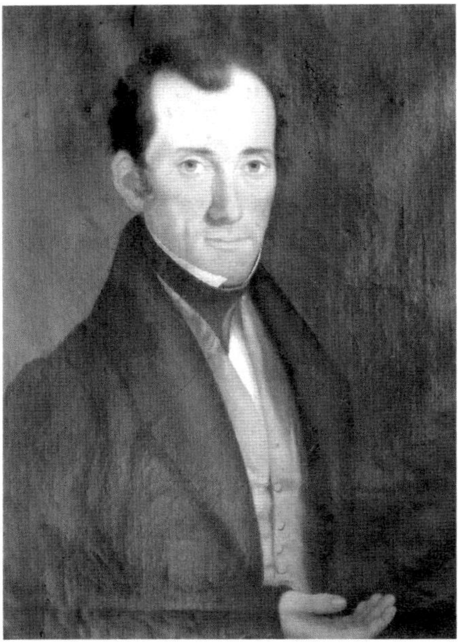

will fight." Ten days later, the Alamo was besieged, and eleven days after that, on March 6, it fell to the enemy. All of the 180 men defending the fort, including Pollard, were killed, but the Texan army went on to win independence.

Today, 150 years later, a portrait of Dr. Amos Pollard hangs in the Alamo Museum to honor the sacrifice of the young man who spent his childhood years in Surry.

Dr. Amos Pollard.

BILL DUNTON FIGHTS THE WAR

Plans to commemorate the 150th anniversary of Civil War battles bring to mind the more than two thousand Cheshire County residents who fought in that war. The experience of one local resident reminds us of the bravery and endurance of these men who volunteered to fight for the Union.

William Dunton of Fitzwilliam was one of the first local men to enlist when the fighting began. He was assigned to the Second Regiment of New Hampshire Volunteers. He was at the First Battle of Bull Run and several other engagements in Virginia in late 1861 and early 1862. The Second Regiment was also engaged at the Second Battle of Bull Run, and Dunton was fighting there alongside his comrades on August 29, 1862. Suddenly he was hit in the face by a bullet. The ball entered his right cheek, breaking his jaw and his upper teeth and exiting below his left eye. Dunton fell and was left for dead by his comrades.

Confederate soldiers stripped him of his possessions and most of his clothes and also left him on the field. Dunton's mouth soon began to fill up from the swelling, and he cut away the torn flesh with his knife so that he could breathe. Hours passed and then days, and still no help came. Finally, six days later, a burial crew found Dunton and carried him to an army hospital at Washington. The surgeons there decided that he could not be saved. To give him a chance, however, a small tube was inserted into his throat through which he was fed. Dunton clung to life and was fed through his tube for more than a month. Finally, two months later, he had recovered enough to be discharged. William Dunton had survived to return to Fitzwilliam and tell the amazing tale of his Civil War experience.

Camp Brooks

In October 1861, the following advertisement appeared in the *New Hampshire Sentinel*: "Now For the Sixth! Wanted, 1000 able-bodied intelligent, temperate, patriotic men for the Sixth Regiment New Hampshire Volunteers…Let old Cheshire show her patriotism by immediately furnishing the men." The Civil War had begun only a few months earlier, but New Hampshire had already put out a call for its sixth regiment of volunteer infantry. It was becoming painfully clear that the war might continue for a long time.

The Sixth Regiment was recruited throughout the state, but more than 230 of its original 885 members were residents of Cheshire County. As soon as the companies were filled, the men were ordered to report to Camp Brooks at Keene. The camp was located at Cheshire Fair Grounds, now the site of Wheelock Park. Nelson Converse of Marlborough was appointed colonel of the regiment, and Simon G. Griffin, a native of Nelson, was made lieutenant colonel.

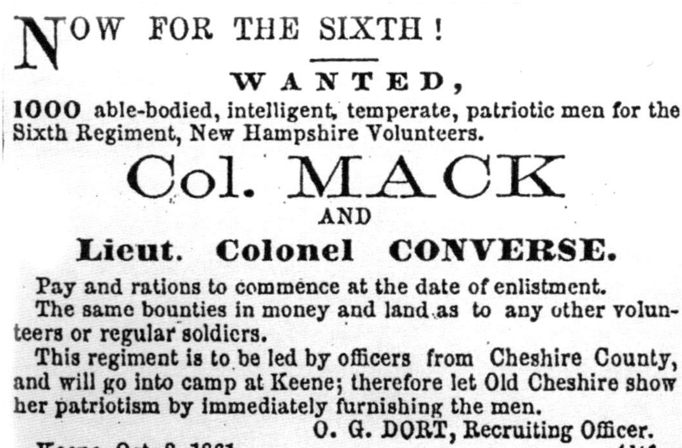

Recruiting advertisement for the Sixth Regiment, New Hampshire Volunteers, 1861.

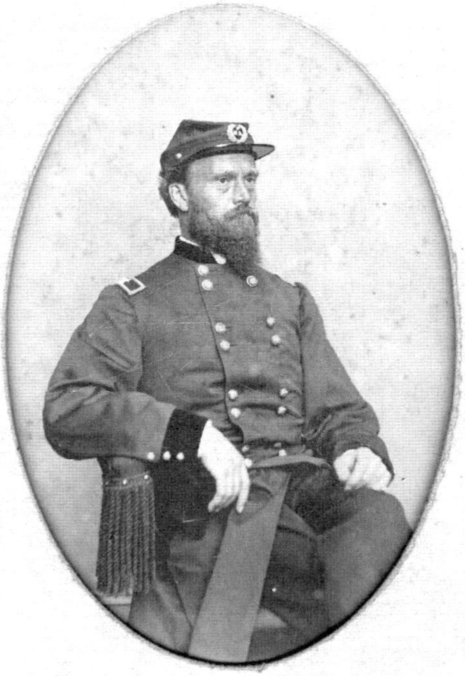

Colonel Simon G. Griffin of the Sixth Regiment.

Howard Rand of Rindge wrote home to his cousin that he had arrived at Camp Brooks on Wednesday, November 26. He was inspected by the surgeon and mustered into the service the following day. The members of the regiment received their enlistment bounties on Friday, and many of the men went into the village where "a good many got tight and made a good deal of disturbance." One of Rand's first military duties was to go downtown and arrest the intoxicated members of his own regiment. He informed his cousin that "[w]e have got our uniform and look like bully soldiers." The ladies of Keene treated the enlistees with a Thanksgiving Day feast. The meal delivered to the camp consisted of turkeys, geese, chickens, puddings, pies, cookies and doughnuts for all of the men. Many residents of the region came to view the activities in camp.

The regiment's last week in Keene was a difficult one as the ground was frozen solid, and the snow was piling up. The men struggled to keep the fires going to warm their large conical tents. On Christmas morning, the soldiers broke camp and marched the one and a half miles from Camp Brooks to the train station through more than a foot of new snow. The *Sentinel* reported that the men were "heartily cheered by an immense crowd that had assembled to witness their departure." The regiment boarded twenty-two cars and rolled off to war, joining General Burnside's expedition to North Carolina two weeks later.

The Sixth Regiment was involved in many of the war's principal battles, including the Second Battle of Bull Run, Antietam, Fredericksburg, the Wilderness, Spotsylvania, and Petersburg. Twenty-two-year-old Howard Rand, who had bragged in his letter to his cousin that he looked like "a bully soldier" after receiving his uniform at Keene in November 1861, sadly lay dead on the battlefield at Antietam, Maryland, ten months later from an enemy bullet to the forehead. Like young Rand, 248 of the original 885 enlistees, 28 percent of the regiment, died in their attempt to preserve the Union.

Stoddard's Unknown Soldier

Although the Robb Cemetery in South Stoddard, New Hampshire, is far from any Civil War battlefield, a young unknown victim of that war was buried there late in 1864. He is buried beside Henry Stevens, another young soldier. It is with Henry Stevens that the story of Stoddard's unknown soldier begins.

Young Henry longed to join the Union army from the beginning of the Civil War in 1861. Five of his older brothers enlisted to serve in the war. One of them died in the service, three were wounded and one was captured by the enemy. It was not until 1864, however, that young Henry could be spared from the family farm in South Stoddard. He enlisted in the Eighteenth New Hampshire Regiment on September 13 of that year.

Henry never made it to the battlefield, however; three weeks later the Stevens family received word that he had died of typhoid fever at a military hospital in New York. His body was sent home and prepared for burial. Soon after the arrival of the coffin, however, a messenger arrived with word that a second coffin, also marked "Private Henry Stevens, Co. A, 18th New Hampshire Volunteers," had arrived at the depot. The first coffin was found to contain the body of a young man unknown to the Stevens family. The second coffin contained the body of young Henry.

Military officials could not identify the stranger, and furthermore, they refused to take him back. Consequently, the Stevens family buried the young stranger in the family lot beside their own son and cared for the stranger's grave as they did for Henry's.

Somewhere the young man's family probably waited many long months and years for word of their loved one, never to learn his fate. Today the grave is marked with a simple granite stone inscribed "U.S. Soldier," and each year on Memorial Day a United States flag is placed on the grave of Stoddard's unknown soldier.

BROTHER AGAINST BROTHER

The Civil War has often been described as the war that saw brother fight against brother. This was truly the case for one Roxbury, New Hampshire family. Six sons were born to Reuben and Rebecca Phillips during the 1820s and early 1830s. Reuben was a deacon in the Nelson Church and an ardent patriot. By 1861, four of the Phillips boys had moved to Missouri and begun new lives there.

When the war began, three of the sons in Missouri—Simeon, Rufus and Judson—supported the Confederate cause. Simeon joined a Confederate regiment, and Rufus and Judson formed a Confederate guerilla company. The fourth son in Missouri, Joseph, joined a Union regiment in that state. Here in New Hampshire a fifth son, Minot, joined the Ninth Regiment of New Hampshire infantry.

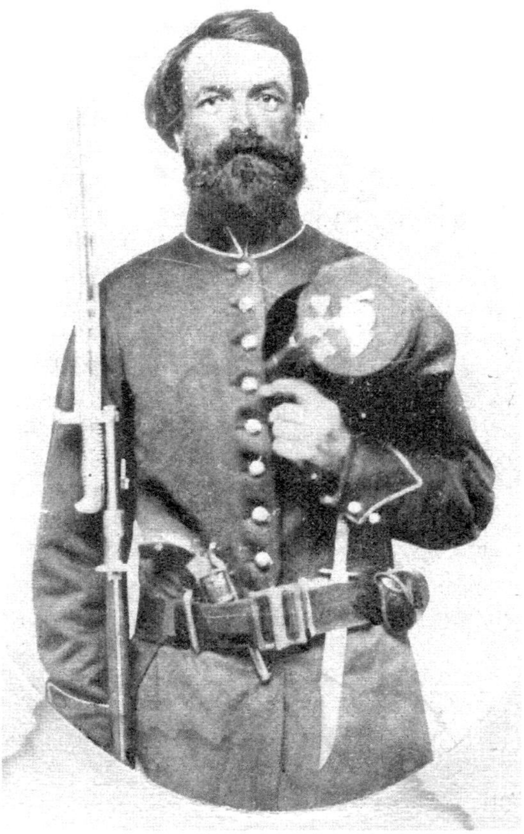

Minot Phillips.

All of the boys saw considerable action in the conflict. Simeon and Rufus, two of the Confederates, were captured and held in Federal prisons. The youngest son, Judson, who was the third of the family's Confederate soldiers, died when he was shot in the head during a skirmish in Missouri.

Both of the brothers who enlisted in the Union army also died. Minot, the son who enlisted in the Ninth New Hampshire Regiment, survived the Battle of Fredericksburg but not its aftermath. He was a member of the detail sent out to bury the dead. The crew dug trenches six feet wide and three feet deep; in each of them they placed and buried up to 275 bodies. The detail worked all day, all night and a second day as well. Upon returning to camp, Phillips and several others were taken sick with typhoid fever. They were sent to a hospital, but Minot succumbed to the disease within a few weeks. Son Joseph died from wounds received in the battle in Helena, Arkansas, in July of the same year. Of the five sons, two were prisoners of war and three died in the service.

There was one more death caused, at least in part, by the war. Reuben, the father, was a firm Unionist. When he heard that three of his sons were with the enemy, he became very upset. He wrote a letter of displeasure to his youngest son Judson and went to the Keene Post Office to mail it. After angrily inserting the letter into the mail slot, Reuben turned to walk away and dropped dead on the post office floor. The Civil War not only claimed the lives of three of the Phillips brothers and resulted in two others being imprisoned, it also claimed the life of their father, far from the fighting, at home in Cheshire County.

Dennie Farr Comes Home

Dennie W. Farr was born in Chesterfield in January 1840. He was the fifth of ten children of Worcester and Abial Farr. His father was a farmer and stonemason in Chesterfield.

Dennie Farr married Mary Brown of Brattleboro and moved to that town, where he was working as a store clerk when the Civil War began. He enlisted in the Fourth Regiment Vermont Volunteers in September 1861 and was commissioned second lieutenant. The need for troops was so pressing that the regiment was called to Washington before they had a chance to be outfitted. Over the next two years, the Fourth was engaged in more than a dozen battles, including Antietam, Fredericksburg and Gettysburg. Dennie Farr was made captain of Company C late in 1862.

Early in May 1864, the regiment was involved in the Battle of the Wilderness in Virginia. During the battle, the regiment lost more than 40 percent of its men killed or wounded, including almost 70 percent of its officers. Among those was Dennie Farr, who was killed by a shot to the head on May 5. The following morning Farr's brother-in-law, Captain Addison Brown of the Fourth Regiment, saw that he was buried on the battlefield. A piece of a wooden cracker box was carved with the words "Capt. D.W. Farr, Co. C, 4th Vt. Inf."

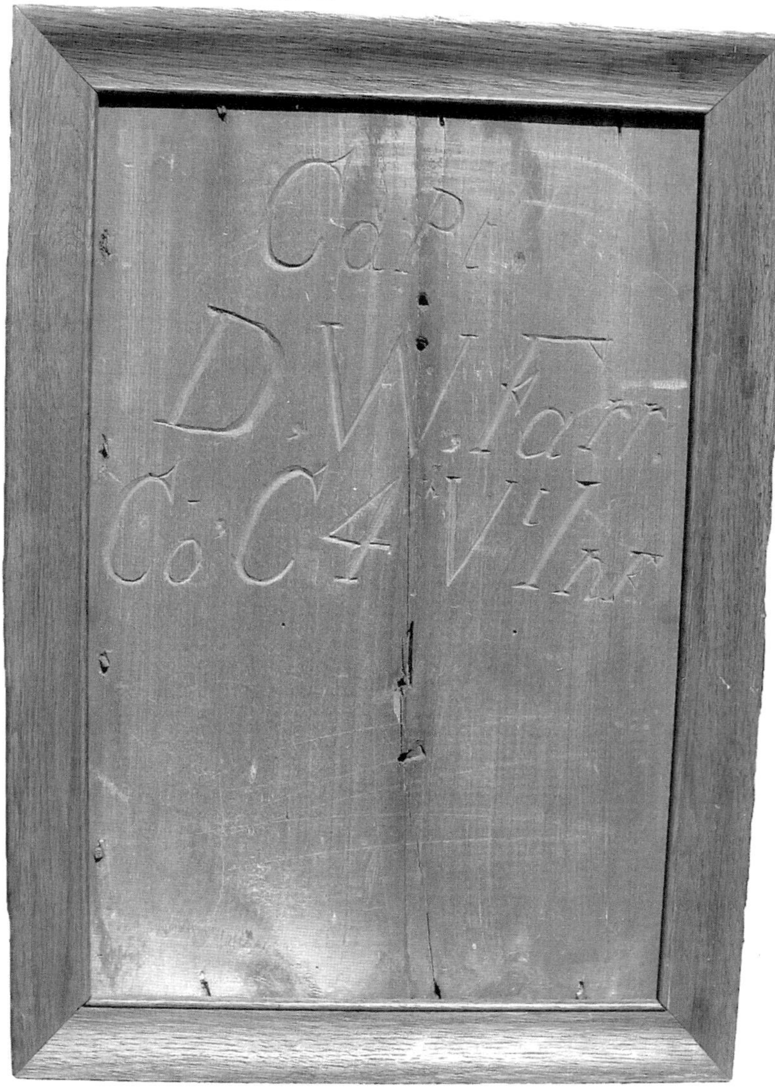

Battlefield grave marker of Captain Dennie W. Farr.

and was placed on the grave. Captain Brown mapped the location of the grave and moved on with the regiment.

The map was delivered to Farr's wife back in Vermont. As soon as possible after the war ended, in May 1865, Captain Farr's wife, accompanied by Captain Brown's wife and Mr. Charles Brown, traveled to the Wilderness battlefield. With the map in hand they found Farr's grave easily. His remains were returned to Chesterfield, where he was reburied with Masonic honors in the West Cemetery. Dennie Farr's temporary wooden grave marker was also brought back and has been preserved to the present day in the collections of the Historical Society of Cheshire County.

The Gallant Ruffle Boys

An item in the "Home and State" column of the *New Hampshire Sentinel* in 1862 reads as follows: "Mrs. Ruffle of Keene has five sons and a son-in-law in the army ready to give their lives for the Union." The American Civil War saw countless families send multiple sons off to fight, but the Ruffle family must have been one of the most active military families in New Hampshire.

Five of Abigail Ruffle's six sons enlisted in the Union army during the first five months of the conflict, three of them within three days in April immediately after the capture of Fort Sumter. Charles, Samuel, George, Benjamin and Josiah ranged in age from nineteen to thirty-two years; all who were physically able served throughout the entire war.

All five Ruffle boys eventually ended up in the Second Regiment of New Hampshire Volunteers as members of Company A and Company H. Their regiment saw action in some of the leading engagements of the war, including Bull Run, Fredericksburg, Gettysburg, Cold Harbor and Petersburg. George was shot in the hand at the Second Battle of Bull Run and discharged disabled. Benjamin was wounded at Gettysburg on July 2, 1863, but reenlisted the following year. Samuel died of typhoid fever in the military hospital at David's Island, New York, in August 1862.

The Ruffle boys' brother-in-law, Cyrus McClure, husband of their sister Isabella, also served in the war. He enlisted in the Sixth Regiment in November 1861. He was appointed second lieutenant in January 1864, wounded at Spotsylvania four months later and discharged due to disability.

By the time the war ended in 1865, the five Ruffle boys had combined to give more than fourteen years of military service for their country. Their mother Abigail saw four of her five soldier sons return from the army. Only Samuel, who was buried near the hospital in New York where he died, did not return home to Cheshire County.

ARLON ATHERTON'S DRUMMER BOY

Arlon S. Atherton of Richmond, New Hampshire, enlisted for service in the Civil War during the summer of 1861 at the age of nineteen years. Arlon Atherton was involved in all fifteen of his regiment's engagements from November of 1861 to the middle of 1864. The depleted regiment, numbering just over two hundred men, was at Deep Bottom, Virginia, in August 1864. On August 16, they were sent to the front lines. Throughout the day, they advanced through woods and fields, engaging the enemy several times and taking three hundred Confederate soldiers prisoner.

Just as the regiment received orders to retreat, Sergeant Atherton was shot through the right lung. He was left for dead on the field because of the apparently mortal nature of his wound. When Atherton regained consciousness, there was a Confederate drummer boy at his side. The boy offered water and did what he could to make his enemy comfortable. Atherton lay on the field for two days; he was vomiting blood, and the Confederates also felt he would not live. Every time he awoke, the boy was there at his side. Most of Atherton's clothing was stolen, and the young drummer boy built a fire to keep him warm at night.

After two days, the Confederates finally removed Atherton from the field and took him to Libby Prison. Once again his wound was ignored, and he was told that he could not live until morning. Finally, after several days, the wound was treated and Atherton recovered enough to be paroled on September 12. After he was removed from the field, however, he did not see the young Confederate soldier who had helped him. Atherton recovered from his wound, rejoined his regiment and served until the end of the war.

Arlon Atherton often thought about the drummer boy who had saved his life despite the fact that they served in opposing armies. In the early 1890s, he sent a letter to the *Richmond Times* outlining his experiences. The Virginia newspaper published the letter, as did newspapers throughout the South. Atherton soon received a letter from J.W. Southward, an inspector at the customhouse in Richmond, who had been a member of the Twenty-second Regiment of Virginia Infantry. Southward related a similar experience that he had had as a seventeen-year-old Confederate private.

Atherton traveled to Richmond, where the two men met, and Atherton came face to face with the man who had saved his life almost thirty years earlier. The two men visited the battlefield and found the spot where Atherton had fallen. Southward and his family then entertained Atherton in their home. Former enemies J.W. Southward of Richmond, Virginia, and Arlon Atherton of Richmond, New Hampshire, became friends because a young Confederate drummer boy had shown compassion for a wounded Union soldier on a battlefield of the American Civil War.

Knight's Gallant Charge

Although many thousand New Hampshire men fought in our country's Civil War, only forty-six of these men earned the nation's highest military award, the Congressional Medal of Honor. Only one of these forty-six men, Charles H. Knight, was a resident of Cheshire County.

Charles Knight was born in Keene and was a twenty-three-year-old resident of the town when he enlisted to fight in the Civil War in 1862. Knight served as a corporal with Company I of the Ninth New Hampshire Regiment of Infantry. On July 30, 1864, the Ninth Regiment was engaged in the Battle of the Crater during the siege of Petersburg. During the battle, the regiment charged the Confederate line. Knight and a Sergeant Simonds led the charge. They were far in front of the other Union soldiers. Just before they reached the enemy line, Knight was shot in the hand and Sergeant Simonds was wounded and fell. Knight continued on, however, and was the first man over the enemy works, where he single-handedly took several prisoners.

After the battle, Knight was taken to a hospital in Washington. The thumb and index finger on his right hand were amputated, and he could not close the remaining fingers. He could no longer fight, and at the age of twenty-five Knight was discharged from the service and went home to Keene.

In 1865, Knight's commanding general, John G. Parke, recommended Knight for the Medal of Honor for courage and gallantry during the Battle of the Crater. No action was taken, however, and the recommendation was made again in 1887. Finally, on July 27, 1896, almost exactly thirty-two years after the battle, Charles H. Knight received the only Medal of Honor awarded to a Civil War veteran from Cheshire County.

THE MURDER OF CAPTAIN RIPLEY

Theodore Ripley was born in Winchester, New Hampshire, in 1835. He grew up in the town and enlisted in the Union army there in August 1862. He helped to organize Company F of the Fourteenth New Hampshire Regiment. He was elected captain of the company and served throughout the war, including at the Battle of Opequan.

Ripley did not return to Winchester after the war but instead went to Georgia, where he worked as superintendent of a lumber plantation. Late on the evening of July 23, 1866, four men arrived at the Ripley home in Georgia. They called Ripley to the front gate and then shot him dead. Because Ripley was a northerner working in the South shortly after the war, the murder was blamed on the Ku Klux Klan. It was nearly a century before the true story behind his death became public, however.

According to documents written by members of the Fourteenth Regiment, many of the enlisted men disliked Ripley because of his tyrannical behavior and harsh discipline. The men put up with two years of this harsh treatment before an incident occurred that they could not forgive. According to a former soldier, an intoxicated Ripley ordered his men to charge "double time" across an open field into a hail of enemy bullets at the Battle of Opequan in Winchester, Virginia. Fifty-three men were killed and ninety were wounded within a few minutes' time.

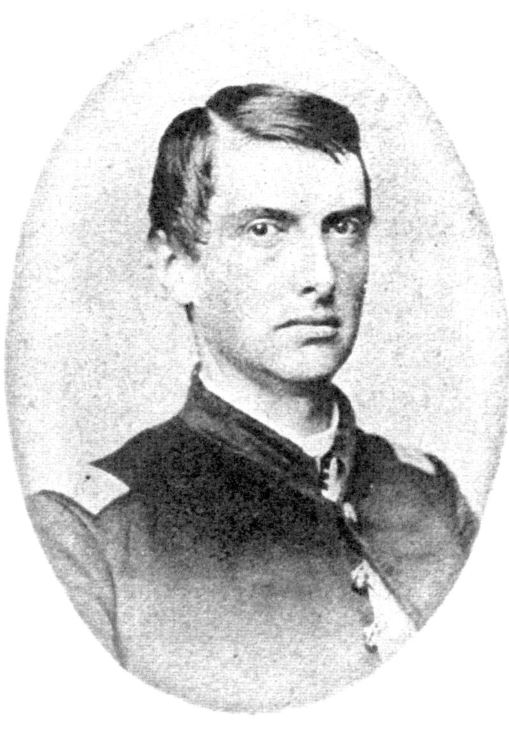

Captain Theodore Ripley.

The true story of Ripley's fate was secretly passed down through the years until it was published in 1960 in a book about the war. It was actually four New Hampshire soldiers who travelled south and met Ripley at the gate of his Georgia home on that fateful evening in July 1866. Ripley's former soldiers had gone there to avenge the painful loss of their fifty-three comrades who had died on the battlefield at Opequan three years earlier.

Rough Rider of Winchester

In 1860, young Charles Wood postponed his medical studies to seek work in a Winchester, New Hampshire sash and blind factory. It was there, in a Main Street apartment above the post office, that Winchester's most notable son, Leonard Wood, was born in October 1860.

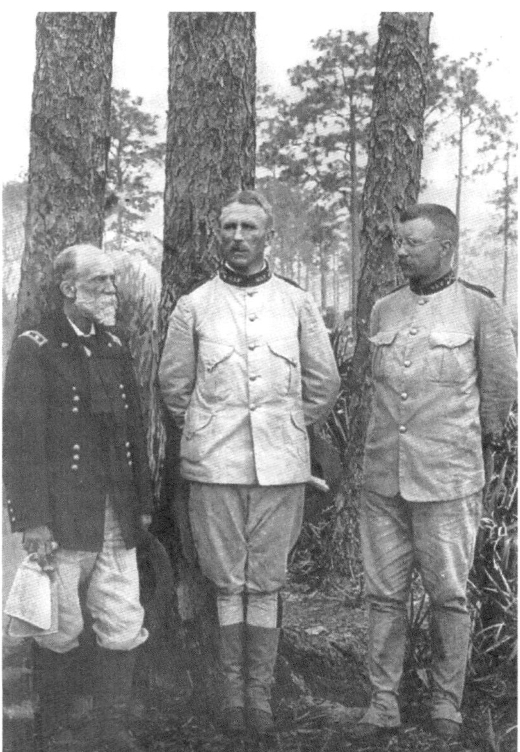

Leonard Wood, center, with General Joseph Wheeler and Colonel Theodore Roosevelt in Cuba.

Leonard Wood's family left Winchester soon after his birth; he spent his boyhood years on Cape Cod. Wood entered Harvard University in 1880 and became the house surgeon at Boston City Hospital upon graduation. Wood soon joined the military as a surgeon with the Geronimo Campaign in Arizona. He won the Medal of Honor before age thirty and remained in the military.

At the outbreak of the Spanish-American War, Wood and his friend Teddy Roosevelt organized the First United States Volunteer Cavalry Regiment, better known as the Rough Riders. Together Wood and Roosevelt led the famous charge up San Juan Hill. Wood gained the rank of general and remained as governor of Cuba when the fighting ended. He cleaned up and civilized the city of Santiago with innovative health ordinances. General Wood also served as governor of the Philippines, was the originator of military training camps in the United States and his name was placed in nomination at the Republican presidential convention in 1920. The nomination was eventually won by Warren G. Harding, who went on to win the presidency.

Although he received three Distinguished Service medals, authored dozens of books and articles and was awarded honorary doctorates by fifteen universities, Winchester native Leonard Wood is best remembered for riding alongside Teddy Roosevelt as they led the charge of the Rough Riders up San Juan Hill.

WORLD WAR HERO

During July 1918, World War I was raging in the north of France. More than six hundred people from Keene served in the war; twenty-five of those gave their lives for the cause. One of those was Private First Class George Dilboy. Dilboy came to Keene a short time before he enlisted to work in a local shoe factory.

Dilboy was a member of Company H of the 103rd U.S. Infantry. The 103rd was fighting in a major offensive in northeastern France in mid-July 1918. On the afternoon of July 18, Dilboy's platoon gained an objective along a railroad embankment. He and his platoon commander had moved forward to examine the ground beyond them when they were fired upon by a machine gun one hundred yards away. From a standing position on the railroad track, fully exposed to view, Dilboy opened fire but failed to silence the gun. He rushed forward through a wheat field toward the machine gun. Twenty-five yards from the gun he fell with several bullet wounds, his right leg almost severed above the knee. He was not defeated, however, and he continued to fire at the machine gun from a prone position, killing two of the enemy and dispersing the rest of the gun crew. Dilboy died a short time later.

Although he was only one of four million U.S. residents who served, George Dilboy has not been forgotten. He was the only New Hampshire resident to receive the Congressional Medal of Honor during World War I and one of only ninety-four American soldiers to be so honored. In 1931, the city of Keene paid to have its war hero's picture placed alongside those of the other ninety-three Medal of Honor recipients at the U.S. World War I memorial in Paris, France.

Unusual Tales

The Stoddard Duel

The European practice of fighting duels, prearranged fights between two people armed with deadly weapons, was very rare in Cheshire County history. There is at least one duel on record in the region, however; it occurred in the town of Stoddard during the 1790s.

Levi Phelps and Ebenezer Polley were neighbors in the western section of Stoddard that is known as "Leominster Corner." Some argument arose between the two men, possibly concerning land boundaries. The dispute was carried to such an extreme that Phelps challenged Polley to a duel, and Polley accepted. Two other neighbors, Nathaniel Evans and David Joslin, were chosen as seconds. Muskets were the weapons of choice. Phelps and Polley insisted on seeing the guns loaded with powder and balls. However, the seconds secretly extracted the balls before giving the muskets to the combatants.

After receiving their instructions, the two men took their positions, marched the prescribed distance, turned and fired. The gunpowder roared but there were no balls to fly. The duelists were amazed that neither was killed or wounded. Phelps and Polley were persuaded to sit down together for a drink, and the two men reconciled over a few mugs of flip.

Although both men escaped unharmed on that day in the 1790s, Levi Phelps lost his life before the decade ended when he drowned in the Connecticut River. Ebenezer Polley left Stoddard at about the same time, but the story of their duel remains alive in Stoddard today more than two hundred years later.

Conjuror Ballou

James Ballou Jr. was born in 1761. His family moved to Richmond, New Hampshire, when he was a youngster. He lived there the rest of his life. During his years in Richmond, Ballou became known far and wide for his ability to foretell the future. Many years later, Ballou's grandson, President James A. Garfield, nicknamed Ballou "the conjuror" when he was gathering family genealogy.

Garfield interviewed many people who recalled his grandfather's ability to foretell the future or determine the location of lost or stolen property. Visitors traveled from a fifty-mile radius around Richmond to have Ballou tell their fortunes. He made his powers seem even more mystical by wearing a wizard's robe and writing out his formulas with geometrical figures that no one else could understand. Ballou predicted important events, led bewildered owners to their missing farm tools and told young couples the direction of their future years.

James Ballou's most amazing forecast, however, was the prediction of his own death. His calculations indicated that he would die on April 30, 1808. His neighbors knew about this prediction and questioned Ballou about his health when the day arrived. He admitted that he was perfectly healthy and that perhaps he had made an error in his calculations.

As he started home from a visit to the blacksmith shop on that fateful day, James Ballou encountered some workmen removing stones from a field. They were struggling with a heavy boulder, and he stopped to assist. Ballou added his strength to the effort and suddenly burst an artery. He was carried home to bed and died before the day was over.

The Gilsum Witch

We generally associate the belief in witchcraft with Salem, Massachusetts, three centuries ago. The belief in witches was widespread throughout New England for several generations, however, and Cheshire County was no exception.

At about the turn of the century in 1800, an elderly woman named Mrs. Rice lived in the town of Gilsum. Some of the townspeople apparently felt that old Mrs. Rice was somewhat unusual and began to circulate strange and fearful stories about her. It was soon commonly believed that she had supernatural powers. One story circulated that several people had seen her pass by over a light snow without leaving any footprints or other sign of her passage.

At one time, a Gilsum woman lay ill with an undiagnosed illness. It was the general belief that she had been bewitched by Mrs. Rice. Dr. Munroe came from Surry but could find no cause for the woman's illness. He was told about the gossip that the woman had been bewitched. The doctor then bled the patient and threw the blood into the fire. The sick woman improved immediately. At about the same time, Mrs. Rice was found to have terrible burns on her hands. This was final proof of her supernatural powers to many townspeople. John Mark scoffed at the rumors, however. He declared that he did not believe that she was a witch because he had turned her out of his house once and she had done nothing to him.

The stories continued, but no action was taken against Mrs. Rice. She apparently lived out her days with the reputation among many of her neighbors of being the witch of Gilsum.

Caring For the Old Folks

In the days before nursing homes, our ancestors had a practical method of caring for the elderly. Parents would give their property to their children on the condition that the parents would be cared for in their home throughout their lives. These conditions were outlined very specifically in the deeds and offer an interesting view of life in the nineteenth century.

Jason Parmenter of Stoddard, for example, deeded his land to his son Asahel in 1802. Asahel was to keep the land if he provided sufficient care for his parents throughout their lives. The deed outlined exactly what was to be provided. His parents were to have the use of a room in the house and wood sufficient for one fire available at all times. They were also to receive specific amounts of corn, rye, wheat, potatoes, cabbage, carrots and turnips, as well as 60 pounds of tea each year. Furthermore, Asahel was to bring his parents 220 pounds of pork and 200 pounds of good beef annually. Finally, he was to provide the assistance of a doctor whenever needed and a decent burial when dead.

Apparently this system of care worked well for our ancestors. It worked well for Jason Parmenter, at least. He was still alive and well at age seventy-six, and the town historian wrote that Parmenter lived "to a good old age" in the town of Stoddard.

Samuel Jones's Leg

Samuel Jones Jr. was born in Hillsborough, New Hampshire, in 1777. His family was among the first to settle in that town in the 1770s. Samuel and several of his brothers and sisters eventually settled in Washington, New Hampshire, in about 1800, when Washington was still a part of Cheshire County. It was in Washington that Samuel was involved in an accident for which he is still remembered.

In early July 1804, when Samuel was twenty-six years of age, he was assisting in the moving of a building in Washington. During the job, Samuel's leg became caught between the building and a fence against which the building became lodged. His leg was so severely injured that it was amputated on July 7, 1804.

Apparently there was a belief at the time that indicated that if a severed limb was properly arranged and aligned, there would be less pain in the remaining portion of the limb. Consequently, Samuel prepared his leg properly and had it buried in the town cemetery. He erected a gravestone on the cemetery lot that read: "Capt. Samuel Jones' leg which was amputated July 7, 1804."

Samuel survived the amputation and later moved to Boston and then to Rhode Island, where the rest of him is buried. But his peculiar gravestone, and his leg, remain in the Washington cemetery to this day.

Disaster at the Langdon Church

Late in the spring of 1842, the residents of Langdon set about constructing a new Congregational Church in their village. On May 26 of that year, some forty men gathered to take part in a church raising bee. They all came and offered their skills to help raise the new building. The body of the building was erected on May 26, and the next day the men returned to finish the roof, belfry and steeple.

Apparently certain timbers had not been properly supported during the work of the previous day. As the forty men worked high up on the roof, the entire structure suddenly came down with a crash. Jonas Blood, a longtime resident of the town, was killed instantly. Sixteen others were injured, several with broken limbs and ribs. John Pratt received a fractured skull, and William Garfield was presumed dead and was carried to a nearby house. Garfield soon recovered, however, and lived for many more years.

This accident was a serious blow to the town, but the church members were not defeated. They soon built another church. In contrast to the Langdon church, which stood for one day in 1842, the new building which replaced it has now stood for more than 150 years.

Millerites in Keene

William Miller of New York was the founder of the nineteenth-century religious denomination known as Millerism. After studying the bible, Miller claimed that he had determined the exact date of the second coming of Christ and the end of the world. Miller had many followers throughout New England. These people were to wait on the hilltops at the appointed time to be gathered up into heaven before the world was destroyed. Miller calculated that the world would end on February 15, 1843.

Mr. Miller had both support and opposition in the Keene area. In December 1842, the *Sentinel* printed an article entitled "The Burning of the World in 1843," which denounced his theories. During the same month, however, a group of Millerites led by Mr. Preble, a preacher from Nashua, held ten days of meetings in Keene. They explained Miller's doctrine and attempted to prove the date of the destruction of the world. At the same time, the Reverend Livermore of Keene was delivering lectures disputing the claims.

The great day finally arrived. It is told that several of Miller's followers in Keene disposed of many of their worldly goods, gathered on Beech Hill and waited for the great event to occur. The next morning at daybreak, they quietly walked back to their homes, much dismayed. Miller claimed that he had made a miscalculation and that the world would actually end before March 21, 1844. That day also came and went and the world remained intact. The *Sentinel* printed the following obituary: "Died on Thursday last, March 21, the greatest Humbug of modern times, Millerism, aged about 10 years."

John Gunnison, Western Explorer

John W. Gunnison was born in November 1812 in Goshen, New Hampshire, then a part of Cheshire County. He spent his childhood in that town and attended local grammar schools and nearby academies. He decided on a military career and was accepted at West Point in the spring of 1833.

Gunnison graduated four years later, second in his class of fifty. Following a visit with his parents at Goshen, he began his military duties. He served with General Zachary Taylor subduing the Seminole Indians in Florida, but the climate of the Everglades seriously impaired his health, and he was transferred to the Corps of Engineers. Over the next twelve years, he worked on a series of surveying projects in the West.

In the spring of 1853, Gunnison was promoted to captain and assigned the important duty of surveying a railroad route from the Mississippi River to the Pacific. His exploring party worked westward, arriving in Utah that October. They discovered that the Mormons and the Paiute Indians were at war. On the morning of October 26, 1853, Gunnison and eleven members of the party who were exploring a river near the railroad route were attacked by a band of Paiutes. Captain Gunnison stepped from his tent and was immediately pierced by fifteen arrows. Four of the soldiers escaped. When a rescue party arrived the next morning, the eight who had died were found mutilated; several, including Gunnison, had had their arms cut off at the elbow. The nearly completed survey and Gunnison's papers had been stolen by the Indians but were later recovered. He was buried in a lonely grave at Fillmore, Utah. Monuments have been erected to his memory at Gunnison, Colorado, and in the family cemetery in Goshen. Perhaps the most important memorial is the growing opinion of historians that the name of Captain John Gunnison should be included on the list of the most important and heroic explorers of the American West.

Twitchell Against Tobacco

More than 150 years ago, before it was definitely known that smoking was hazardous to the health, one Keene doctor led the battle against the use of tobacco. Dr. Amos Twitchell was born in Dublin, New Hampshire, in 1781. He became a resident of Keene in 1810. By the 1830s and 1840s, he was highly

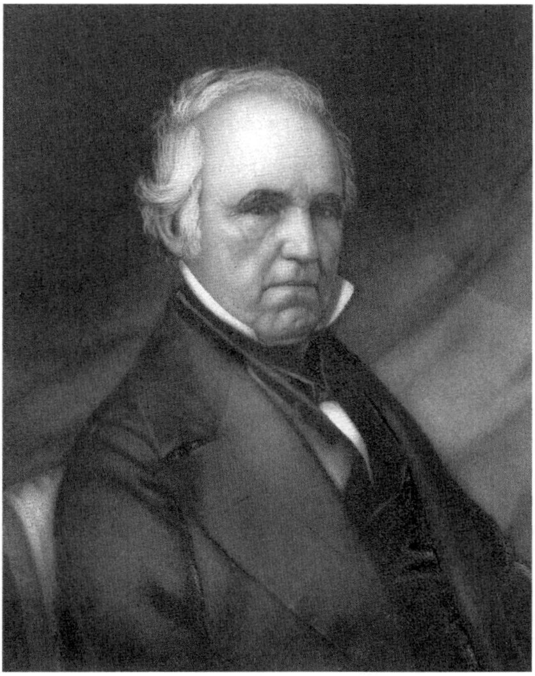

Dr. Amos Twitchell.

respected in his profession. At that time, he gave a lecture on the effects of tobacco on the human system.

In 1842, Dr. Twitchell attributed several health problems to smoking, including heart palpitations, chest pains and severe headaches. He linked heart disease directly to the use of tobacco. He felt that smoking interfered with the respiration and that the lungs were not allowed to do their job properly. As a result, the blood, and consequently the heart, were damaged.

Although Dr. Twitchell had no way of proving his suspicions, he recorded the frequency of chest, heart and respiration problems in his tobacco-chewing and tobacco-smoking patients. He also noted that these symptoms often disappeared entirely when a patient discontinued the use of tobacco. A story about Dr. Twitchell and one of his patients illustrates his views on tobacco use.

One day in his travels, Dr. Twitchell met a farmer from whom he often purchased grain. The farmer looked miserable, and Dr. Twitchell asked about the man's health. The farmer replied, "Almost gone, doctor. I shall never bring you any more corn. The physicians have all given up and tell me I am dying of consumption." Dr. Twitchell said that he was sorry that he would get no more corn, but that he thought he might be able to cure the man. The farmer replied that it was too late and that he must prepare to die.

The doctor offered to make a bargain with the man. The farmer had to agree to follow Twitchell's prescription for three months. If he recovered, he was to pay the doctor fifty bushels of corn, but if he died, the doctor would pay the man's family the equivalent of the corn in cash. After some hesitation, the man agreed. Dr. Twitchell directed the man to take the tobacco from his mouth and never to touch tobacco again in any form.

Six months later, the doctor met up with the man, who was apparently in perfect health, and claimed the corn. The man refused, saying that his wife thought fifty bushels of corn was more than his life was worth. The two compromised, and the farmer gave Dr. Twitchell three or four bushels of corn and a bushel of white beans.

In the late 1840s, one physician read Dr. Twitchell's notes and concluded that "smokers will almost inevitably suffer more or less, and in some instances they will have to undergo an amount of torture to which it seems almost impossible to believe that any man would voluntarily subject himself."

ROSINA DELIGHT RICHARDSON

Samuel Richardson came from Sutton, Massachusetts, to settle in Alstead, New Hampshire, in the late 1700s. His descendants remained there for several generations. The Richardson men were well known and respected in Alstead, but the Richardson women have generally been forgotten and ignored in the local history books. One of the Richardson girls made a name for herself, however, and was well known and remembered by thousands of American children.

Records indicate that Rosina Delight Richardson was born in Alstead in the 1830s. The town of Marlow has also claimed Rosina as a native, and the Richardsons did indeed own property there. In any case, Rosina Delight arrived as a five-pound baby girl in April 1833.

Rosina was different from the other children. She soon grew larger than her young friends…and larger, and larger. When Rosina went to the store in the village, she had to go around the back and enter through the wide grain room door. At home she sat on two chairs. At school the town school committee had to have the desk in front of Rosina removed so that she had space to sit down and do her lessons. By the age of nineteen Rosina Delight had grown to 515 pounds.

It was at about that time that Rosina left home to find fame and fortune. She measured five feet, three inches tall and five feet, three inches around the waist. It is said that she eventually weighed more than 750 pounds. Rosina Delight Richardson of Alstead was soon known across the nation, as she became P.T. Barnum's most famous "fat lady of the circus."

"He Perished of Cold"

In 1864, Jonathan Whittier moved with his family into a sixty-year-old farmhouse in the southwest corner of Stoddard, New Hampshire. Jonathan worked the farm and renovated the old farmhouse. In the mid-1870s, as he approached sixty years of age, it is said that he worked the fields like a man half his age.

On December 29, 1876, Jonathan walked to the post office in Munsonville, some three miles distant, to pick up the family's mail. Snow began to fall as he made his journey. He picked up his mail and started toward home. The storm changed to a blizzard, and the snow piled up fast and deep. Jonathan Whittier never returned home to his farm that evening.

When the weather cleared, Jonathan's family began searching for him. They found that he had started home from the post office, but they could find no trace of him anywhere in the neighborhood. For three months, the family waited, with no word of their husband and father.

On March 25, 1877, as the winter snows began to melt, Jonathan's body was found by the roadside, not far from his home. His gravestone in the Munsonville Cemetery recounts the tale of his tragic death. It reads: "Jonathan H. Whittier, died December 29, 1876, age 58 years, 8 months. He perished of cold by the wayside in trying to reach his home. Found March 25, 1877."

Shooting the Falls

We have all heard of the numerous attempts, both successful and unsuccessful, to shoot, or go through, Niagara Falls. Closer to home, here in Cheshire County, however, the residents of North Walpole and Bellows Falls know of several people who have gone through the falls between these two villages on the Connecticut River.

One of the most publicized trips through the falls was that of Captain Paul Boyton on October 30, 1879. Captain Boyton was on a pleasure trip down the Connecticut at the time. He arrived at Bellows Falls at nightfall and decided that he would go through the falls the next morning. Word of the daring feat spread through the countryside, and two thousand spectators gathered on the bridges and the riverbanks early the next day.

The water was quite high and rushed through the narrow gorge of the falls with great force. Boyton donned a rubber floating suit and paddled into the river above the falls. The current carried him toward the gorge. He became caught in several whirlpools and had to fight diligently to escape them. He was finally carried into the narrow gorge with great speed and disappeared. He did not reappear for some time as the spectators watched anxiously. Boyton finally reappeared well down river and made his way to the shore.

He stayed at a hotel in Bellows Falls that evening and recounted his experience to an attentive audience. He stated that the water pushed him down to the bottom of the channel, and he was sure he was about to die. Boyton said that it was the worst experience he had ever had and that nothing would persuade him to repeat his trip over Bellows Falls.

TURNED TO STONE

Charles Emery was a twenty-year-old Jaffrey resident when he enlisted to fight with New Hampshire's Fourteenth Regiment during the Civil War. One year later, he died of disease at Washington, D.C. His body was sent home, and young Charles was buried in the family plot in Conant Cemetery in Jaffrey.

Fourteen years later, in 1876, the Emery family decided to rearrange the plot, and Charles's body was uncovered for this purpose. Imagine the surprise of those involved when they uncovered the body and saw that Charles's features, clothing and the flower wreath in the coffin were perfectly preserved and appeared just as they had on the day of the burial. Upon investigation, it was discovered that Charles was petrified; his body had turned to stone. The *New Hampshire Sentinel* reported that although Charles weighed 125 pounds when he was alive, his body now weighed some 600 to 700 pounds.

Organic material can be petrified, or turned into a stony replica, when it is impregnated with dissolved chemicals. This is what happened to Charles. A similar case was reported in Stoddard twenty years earlier when the body of one-year-old Clarissa Gerould was moved to a different plot forty years after her death and was found to be petrified. Cases such as these must have been a shock to our ancestors who had reason to exhume their loved ones and found them appearing much as they did when they died many years earlier.

The Amazing Case of Phineas Gage

During the late 1840s, a railroad was built from Bellows Falls to Burlington, Vermont, to connect with the Cheshire Railroad and other rail lines to Boston. During construction near Bellows Falls, an accident occurred that was viewed as one of the most remarkable cases in medical history.

In September 1848, Phineas Gage was supervising some rock blasting to clear the way for the railroad. Gage was powdering a hole when, assuming his assistant had placed sand over the blasting powder, he dropped his tamping iron in the hole to pack the powder. The sand had not been applied, however, and the iron rod caused a spark, which ignited the powder and shot the rod from the hole as if shot from a gun. Gage was leaning over the hole. The three-and-a-half-foot-long, one-fourth-inch-diameter rod entered his cheek, passed behind his left eye and through his brain and exited through the top of his head. Gage was knocked flat by the blast, but was able to sit up and talk after a few minutes. He was taken home and attended by a doctor. Gage was able to walk on his own and told the doctor that he hoped he wasn't hurt too badly. Exertions caused hemorrhaging and the loss of additional brain matter, but Gage soon began to heal.

The case became known far and wide, and Gage traveled to Boston several times to visit specialists. On one such trip, he stopped at the Keene depot and exhibited his tamping rod to several local residents. The accident caused blindness, paralysis of the eyelids and psychological changes in the patient, but Phineas Gage lived an otherwise normal life before passing away nineteen years after his accident.

Bad Baseball

Labor Day 1898 promised to be a memorable day for baseball fans in Keene. The Keene team was scheduled to play a double-header against the Hinsdale team on the Riverside grounds near Island Street. Baseball was taken seriously in the region at that time. Hundreds of people turned out for the games, and outside players were brought in to ensure quality teams.

Keene won the first game by a score of 9–7 on that day. The second game had barely begun when Fred Doe, the second baseman for the Hinsdale team, was hit by a pitch. Doe, who had a reputation for losing his temper,

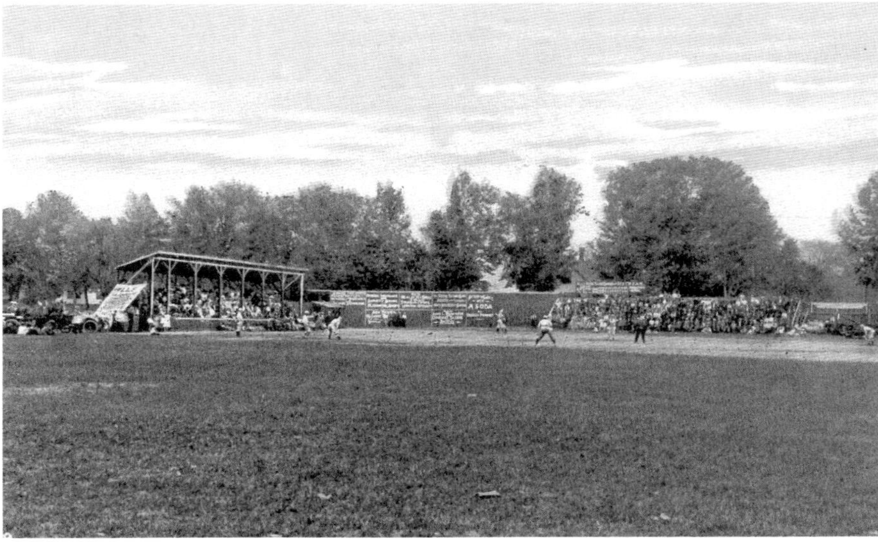

The Island Street ball field in Keene.

threw his bat at Keene pitcher John Griffin. Griffin ducked at the last moment avoiding serious injury as the bat flew over his head. The pitcher started toward the batter's box, where he was met with a violent kick to the stomach from Doe, sending him to the ground.

By this time, the crowd was wild with anger. Two hundred spectators left the stands and chased Doe across the field. The gatekeeper closed the door behind Doe, slowing the pursuing crowd. They soon made their way through, however, and chased Doe down Island Street, where he hid at the home of Thomas Finan. Mrs. Finan locked the doors as the crowd arrived. The police soon arrived, quieted the crowd and arrested Doe. He was charged with assault and battery and fined $12.45, which he paid. Doe then hired a wagon and left town before the crowd left the ball field that afternoon. Griffin, the Keene pitcher, was able to finish the game, although it took him several minutes to recover from the attack. Keene won the game 5–3, sweeping the double-header.

There was a happy ending to this otherwise sad tale. The Thomas Finan family of Island Street enjoyed a Thanksgiving feast that year. Fred Doe sent Mrs. Finan a twenty-five-pound turkey as thanks for hiding him from two hundred angry Keene fans on Labor Day 1898.

The Village that Disappeared

The town of Roxbury near the center of Cheshire County is one of the smallest in size and has been among the smallest in population in the region. This small section of the county is hilly and isolated from the town centers of the surrounding communities. As a result, the residents of the area applied for incorporation as a separate town in 1812, and Roxbury was formed from parts of the towns of Keene, Nelson and Marlborough.

A church was built and a village grew up around it. Roxbury Center village became the home of a tavern, store, blacksmith shop and center school. Several homes, a parsonage and the Roxbury Post Office were also located in the neighborhood. Many of the residents were farmers, but there was a sawmill down the hill and a granite quarry just down the road. By 1820, the population had grown to 366.

By the middle of the nineteenth century, however, the town had begun to decline. The population dropped to 260 by 1850 and to 126 by 1880. The younger generations found that the rocky land was not suited for farming, and many young men moved west to find richer soil. Because of the isolation, which had brought the village into being, large-scale industry was not practical. The former tavern was moved to Marlborough in the 1890s, homes were removed or disappeared and the school was no longer used. The little church in the heart of the village survived the longest. It finally

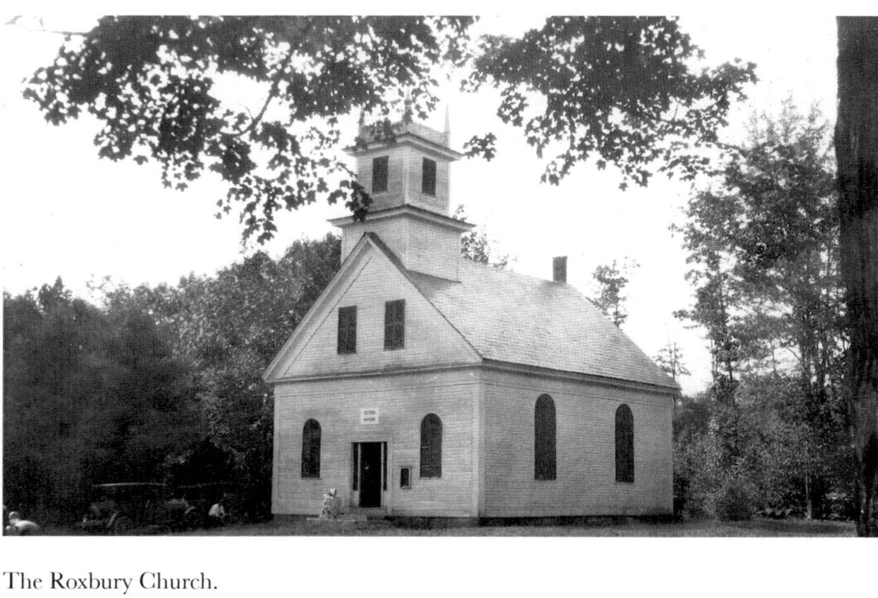

The Roxbury Church.

stood alone in a small clearing where the village had previously been. Finally, in a state of disrepair, the church itself was removed in 1959, and the village of Roxbury disappeared from the maps but not from the memories of those who had known it.

THE FIREPROOF HOUSE

Fred Sharby had a new home constructed on Roxbury Street in Keene in the late 1930s. Sharby owned a chain of motion picture theatres in Massachusetts, New Hampshire and Vermont at that time.

Fred Sharby had a fear of fires; two of his big theatres had burned to the ground. Consequently, when he designed a new home for his family, he made it fireproof. The new house had a stucco exterior, steel support girders, plaster walls and ceilings, tile floors and iron doors. Sharby and his wife and four children moved into the house in 1939.

One of those children, Fred Sharby Jr., soon became the star of the Keene High School football team. During the autumn of 1942, the Boston College football team was ranked first in the country. Sharby decided to take his son to see the Boston College Eagles play Holy Cross in late November of that year. Mr. and Mrs. Sharby and Fred Jr. attended the game with Fred's girlfriend and her parents.

Following the big game, the group went to a Boston nightclub for dinner. They were enjoying dinner and dancing when a fire broke out in the restaurant that night. Young Fred's mother and his girlfriend were the only two of the group of six from Keene to survive the tragic fire. It was more than six decades ago that Fred Sharby, the man with the fireproof home, died along with almost five hundred others in the famous Cocoanut Grove fire in Boston.

Education

No College at Winchester

Winchester, New Hampshire, was a rapidly growing town of approximately five hundred residents by the late 1760s. It was at that time that Dr. Wheelock of Connecticut was searching for a location for his new college. According to a report dated December 1768, the Reverend Ebenezer Cleveland was sent to New Hampshire to scout out towns for the school. He reported that he spent several days with gentlemen in the lower towns of New Hampshire discussing this project. One of these towns was apparently the thriving village of Winchester.

According to several historic sources, Josiah Willard, one of Winchester's leading residents and principal landowners, refused to allow the college to be located there. He feared that the presence of a college would depreciate the value of land in Winchester. Colleges were not always viewed as a positive influence 250 years ago. Students were often viewed as bothersome if not downright immoral.

The agents for the new school bypassed Winchester and continued their search. Dr. Eleazer Wheelock eventually located his educational institution in the wilderness at Hanover, New Hampshire. He called the new school Dartmouth College.

CHESTERFIELD ACADEMY

The *New Hampshire Register* of 1811 listed the Chesterfield Academy as one of only twelve academies in the state. Academies were private secondary schools and were virtually the only means of obtaining a secondary education in New Hampshire at the time. The Chesterfield Academy had actually been founded in 1790 and was the first academy in this section of the state. It had an excellent reputation during its early years, being ranked second only to Phillips Exeter.

Seventy to one hundred students were usually in attendance. They were mostly local residents, but many came from Vermont and Massachusetts as well. The by-laws set the tuition at twenty-five cents per week, and unexcused absences were to be punished by a twenty-five-cent fine for each day absent. Students were forbidden to use indecent language, keep cards or dice or visit public houses. They were also to keep themselves neat and clean and were not to dispute or contradict the principal.

Many students went on to distinguished careers after their stay at Chesterfield, including several who became prominent lawyers and

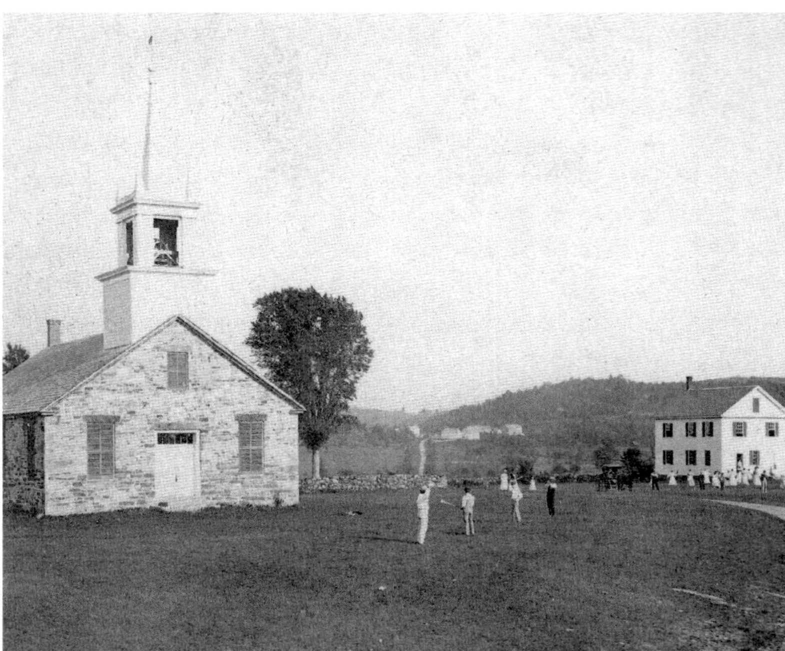

Students in the yard of the Chesterfield Academy, seen on the right, with the town hall on the left.

doctors. Among the more famous graduates were Reverend Hosea Ballou, pioneer of Universalism; Dr. Horace Wells, inventor and pioneer in the field of anesthesia; famed surgeon Amos Twitchell; and Governor William Haile.

The school realized its greatest prosperity during the 1820s, when Chesterfield was one of the leading towns in the county with a population greater than that of Keene. Public high schools began to predominate in the middle of the nineteenth century, however, and academies began to lose their importance. The Chesterfield Academy continued on for many years, but after 1850 it lost the previous prominence that had made it one of the most distinguished educational institutions in New Hampshire.

Young Ladies Seminary

A female teacher named Catharine Fiske arrived in Keene in 1811, where she opened a private school for young women on the town's Main Street. This was one of the first schools in the United States dedicated to women's education.

Public high schools were rare at the time. Education beyond the eighth-grade level was undertaken in private academies and seminaries, such as Catharine Fiske's Young Ladies Seminary in Keene. Most of the advanced education in the early nineteenth century was designed for young men, who were expected to go on to become the doctors, lawyers and ministers of the young nation. Fiske believed that young women had at least as much right to higher education as men. It was their responsibility, as mothers and classroom teachers, to educate the boys and girls who would lead the nation in all walks of life.

Fiske's school was a great success and operated for thirty years. More than 2,500 students from Maine to Michigan to Florida attended the seminary. In addition to the polite classes in music, drawing and painting, the students studied English, geography, history, logic, philosophy, chemistry, Latin, French and numerous other subjects. The school gained a national reputation. It was recognized in national publications of its day for its quality of education and the leadership and educational philosophy of its principal.

When Catharine Fiske died in 1837, the town of Keene literally shut down so that the townspeople could all attend her funeral. Her influence

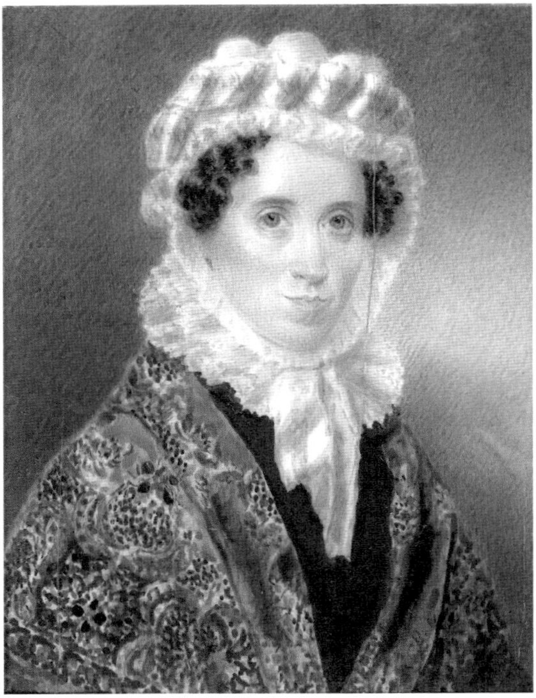

Catharine Fiske.

continued beyond her death, however. The 2,500 females whose lives she had helped to shape went out from this unique school in Keene into hundreds of public classrooms, into the numerous private academies they founded and into the college classrooms where they taught, to help shape the lives of countless young Americans in succeeding generations.

SAMUEL LITCH, SCHOOLMASTER

Samuel Litch was born in Lunenburg, Massachusetts, in 1779. His father died when he was nine years old, and he was sent to live with his grandfather in Vermont. Samuel never attended school as a youngster. After the work on the farm was completed for the day, he studied the few books available to him until late at night.

Litch returned to Massachusetts at the age of eighteen and was able to attend school for the first time. After six weeks of disorder in the classroom, the teacher in the district school was forced to resign. Litch's classmates then elected him as teacher. The school committee agreed; he began teaching and remained in that profession the rest of his life.

Samuel Litch moved to Jaffrey in 1806 and began teaching in the district schools there. He was schoolmaster throughout the town for two decades. His students became so attached that they followed him from district to district so that he would be their teacher.

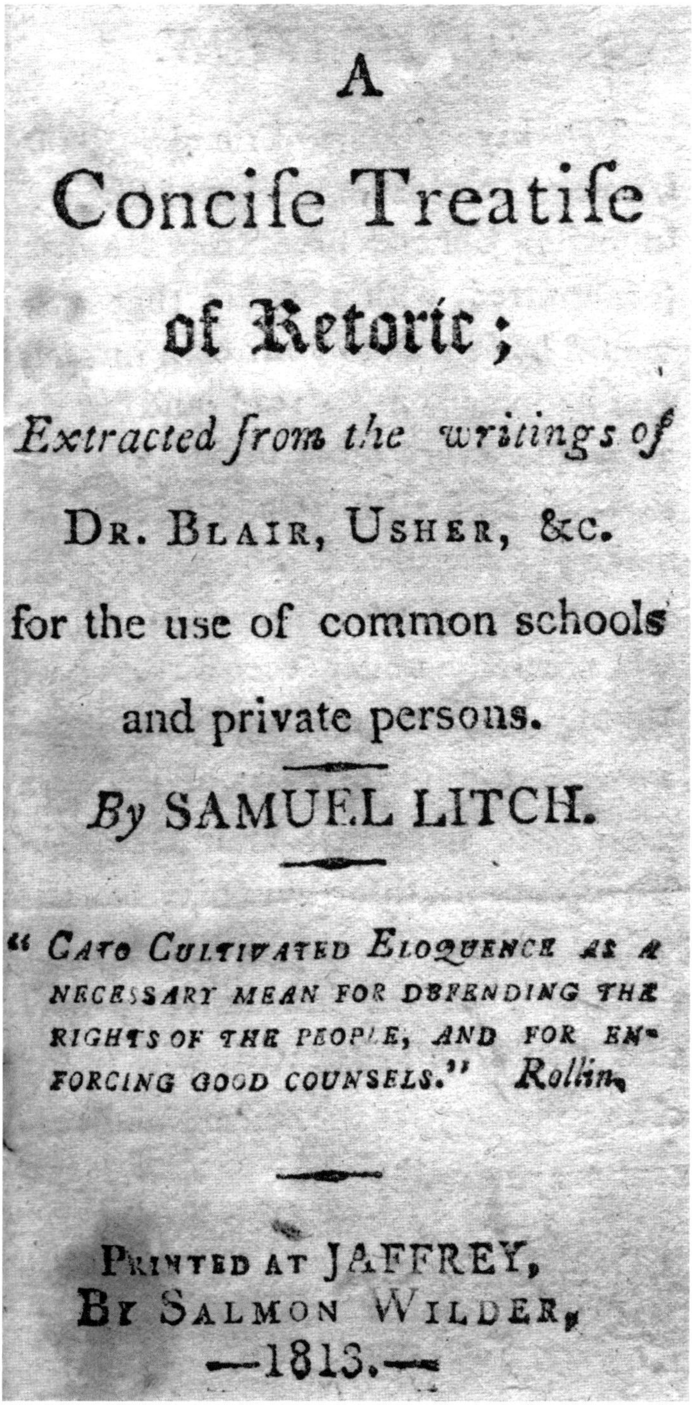

A

Conciſe Treatiſe

of Retoric;

Extracted from the writings of

DR. BLAIR, USHER, &c.

for the use of common schools

and private persons.

By SAMUEL LITCH.

"*CATO CULTIVATED ELOQUENCE AS A NECESSARY MEAN FOR DEFENDING THE RIGHTS OF THE PEOPLE, AND FOR ENFORCING GOOD COUNSELS.*" *Rollin.*

PRINTED AT JAFFREY,
BY SALMON WILDER,
—1813.—

"A Concife Treatife of Retoric" ("A Concise Treatise of Rhetoric") by Samuel Litch.

Litch rose early in the morning and cared for his farm animals before walking several miles to his school. Once there, he built the fire, shoveled the snow, cut the wood, made the pens and then taught as many as one hundred pupils their lessons. In his spare time, he wrote textbooks on rhetoric, geography and other topics. Dedicated schoolmaster Samuel Litch is described modestly in the Jaffrey town history as being "distinguished for discipline and aptness as a teacher."

SAMUEL HALL, EDUCATOR

Samuel R. Hall was born in Croydon, New Hampshire, in 1795. In 1811, the Hall family moved to Rumford, Maine, where Samuel's father had been named pastor of the Congregational Church. Samuel was the youngest of a large family, and there was no money for him to go to college. He had attended Kimball Union Academy, however, and was called on to teach at the local school in Rumford in 1814. This began a long and illustrious educational career for Samuel.

By 1823, Samuel himself had become a minister and was serving the town of Concord, Vermont. During that year, he established a training school for teachers. Prior to that time, educational theory had been discussed a great deal. Samuel, however, took the first practical step by opening his normal school, reputedly the first teacher training school in the United States. It was known as Concord Academy. Samuel went on to teach in other places and organize other teacher training schools. He also wrote some twenty textbooks on geology, geography, arithmetic, grammar and history, as well as the bestseller *Lectures on School-Keeping*, the first American textbook on teaching.

Despite all of these accomplishments, Samuel Hall is probably best remembered today for his invention of a simple yet far-reaching piece of classroom equipment. During 1823, the same year that he founded the Concord Academy, nineteen-year-old Hall patented one of his teaching innovations. The device was a pine board planed smooth and painted black. The board could be written upon with chalk and then erased to be used over and over again. Samuel Hall's invention, known as the blackboard, has been used in nearly every classroom in the United States over the last 175 years.

Animals of All Sorts

Wolves in Croydon

Benjamin Cutting of Worcester, Massachusetts, moved into the wilderness of Croydon, New Hampshire, in the 1700s. Benjamin was one of the early settlers in the town, clearing land and building a rough house for his family on the banks of the Sugar River.

Before his land was fully productive for crops and before any stores were opened in the neighborhood, Benjamin occasionally traveled a long distance to acquire provisions. On one such trip, he was detained over night and all of the next day.

Benjamin's wife and two young children had not eaten in some time and had no food in the house. Mrs. Cutting finally walked to the nearest neighbor's house to ask for food. She had just reached the neighboring homestead when she heard the howling of wolves in the distance. Fearing for the safety of her children, she immediately ran toward home.

The mother soon realized that the wolves were right behind her. Mrs. Cutting arrived at her house and slammed and locked the door behind her, just as the pack of wolves arrived on the other side. Seeing that way blocked, the wolves climbed onto the roof, which was constructed of bark. There was no chimney for the house—only a hole in the roof for the smoke to escape. The frightened mother took her poker and stirred the fire to fill the hole with sparks and flames. The terrible howling of the wolves and their attempts to bite through the roof terrified the family. Whenever one of the wolves showed its face through the hole in the roof,

Mrs. Cutting would greet it with a red-hot poker. She used the contents of her straw bed to feed the flames.

The battle continued through the night. The straw and firewood were almost exhausted when the wolves finally retreated and did not return. The young mother had won the conflict. The family survived, grew and thrived in its new home, and the children and grandchildren of the Benjamin Cutting family became leading citizens of Croydon.

ELEAZER WILCOX AND THE BEAR

Eleazer Wilcox was an early settler of Gilsum, New Hampshire, residing there in the 1770s. One day he met up with a bear in what has become one of the most famous wild animal encounters in the history of the region.

The encounter occurred one early summer day in the year 1776 as Wilcox was on his way to his pasture near the southern border of Gilsum. Along the way, he discovered a large bear, which he shot and wounded. The bear escaped, however, and Wilcox went to Joshua Osgood of Sullivan, who owned a hunting dog, for help in tracking down the wounded animal.

Wilcox and Osgood tracked the bear for three miles before separating to have a better chance for a shot. The wounded bear suddenly charged Wilcox from behind a tree. Wilcox raised his gun, but it misfired. The bear reared up on its back legs, knocked the gun away and took hold of Wilcox. Wilcox seized the bear's tongue and held on with all his strength. The hunting dog continually attacked the bear from the rear, and Wilcox, a large and powerful man, was able to remain on his feet as the bear pressed down upon him. Osgood soon arrived on the scene and carefully took aim and shot the bear, whereupon it released its hold and ran into the woods, where it was found dead the next day.

Wilcox was carried home on a litter and was found to have no less than forty-two wounds upon his body. Amazingly, he recovered and lived for forty-seven more years to the age of seventy-four. He was never completely well, however, and was occasionally subject to illnesses that he called his "bear fits."

The encounter with the bear was a favorite family story for many years. The gun that Wilcox had with him that day is still marked with the deep gouges made by the attacking bear. This trusted firearm has been passed down from generation to generation and was undoubtedly used as evidence to convert nonbelievers in the tale of Eleazer Wilcox and the bear.

Thaddeus Parmenter and the Wolves

Thaddeus Parmenter was an early settler of Marlborough, New Hampshire, arriving there from Sudbury, Massachusetts, in 1789. He soon married and began to build a homestead and raise a family.

One day a short time after he settled in town, Thaddeus carried a load of grain to the gristmill of Daniel Gould. Several other customers had arrived at the mill before young Thaddeus, and he had to wait some time to have his grinding done.

It was nearly nighttime when Thaddeus headed for home, and darkness soon descended upon him. He was startled by the barking of wolves as he neared his home. Pausing on the trail, Thaddeus saw some twenty wolves coming toward him, following the scent that he had left on his way to the mill. With only a moment to act, Thaddeus threw his bag of meal into the woods and followed it by jumping as far as he could into the underbrush. He picked up a branch for protection, crouched down on the ground and waited. Within a few moments, the lead wolf reached the spot from which Thaddeus had leaped. The wolves paused for a moment as Thaddeus held his breath a few feet away. The wolves found the scent fresher where Thaddeus had just come from the mill, and they quickly continued in that direction, not noticing him in the bushes.

He picked up his bag and started toward home as soon as the wolves were out of sight, fearing that they might return. Thaddeus arrived at home safely, where he found his wife in despair. She had heard the wolves and feared that he would not return. Following this experience, Thaddeus Parmenter always went to the mill in the morning and returned home before dark.

P.T. Barnum's Woolly Wonder

In 1842, the famous circus showman P.T. Barnum made an announcement that a special expedition to the wild Rocky Mountains had captured "a new wonder of the world, strange and unique beyond description." This new wonder was a horse covered with wool, like sheep's wool, rather than hair. Barnum announced that the horse would soon be delivered to his New York museum for exhibition.

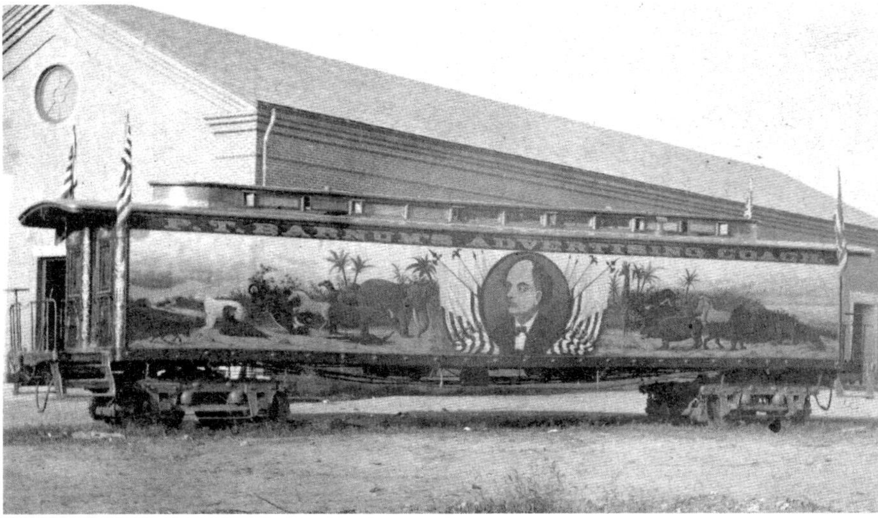

P.T. Barnum's advertising coach in the Keene rail yards.

While Barnum's claim that the horse was covered with a woolly looking substance was true, his publicity about the creature's capture in the wild Rockies was not quite accurate. In truth, the horse was born and bred on the farm of a Mr. Goodrich of Chesterfield, New Hampshire. Goodrich sold the horse to John Stearns, a horse dealer from Hinsdale. Stearns kept the horse on his farm and frequently used the animal to drive in to the village. Word of the freak reached Barnum, and he purchased the horse for $100.

Barnum delayed delivery of the woolly wonder to New York for several weeks so that he could properly arouse the public with his fantastic publicity, including the statement that the horse had been captured "at the risk of life and limb among the snow-capped impassable crags of the wildest mountains in America." In a short time, the woolly creature was quietly delivered from Hinsdale to New York, where P.T. Barnum undoubtedly realized a handsome profit on his $100 investment.

THE DEATH OF THE ELEPHANT "ALBERT"

During July 1885, the Barnum, Bailey and Hutchinson Circus came to Keene. The circus came to town often during those times, but this visit was unlike any other Keene would ever experience.

The circus had been at Nashua before coming to Keene. During the afternoon show at Nashua, Barnum's famous elephant Albert attacked another large bull elephant. Several animal keepers tried to stop the fight. Albert seized one of the keepers, James McCormack, and hurled him to the ground. Albert then pressed McCormack against the ground with his head before turning and running from the tent. The elephant was quieted by his trainer, but McCormack had been badly injured by the weight of the animal. McCormack refused to go home or stay at Nashua and started for Keene on the train with the circus. Before the train arrived, however, McCormack died of internal injuries.

Mr. Hutchinson, one of the show's proprietors, arrived in Keene soon after the train. He determined that Albert showed signs of insanity and had to be done away with. He arranged to have Albert shot by thirty members of the Keene Light Guard. Despite attempts to keep the shooting quiet, the news spread quickly throughout the city. Although the circus was showing on that July day, five hundred people gathered in another location, along the banks of the Ashuelot River, where Albert had been tied to a tree. The guardsmen arrived, and Albert died immediately when the thirty shots rang out. The Smithsonian Institution accepted the gift of the dead elephant and sent two men to recover it. An inscribed marble marker was erected to Albert's memory on the site of the execution. Souvenir hunters chipped off pieces of the stone, and it soon disappeared entirely. The exact site of the death of Albert, the famous show elephant, has now been lost and forgotten.

Austin Corbin's Park

Austin Corbin, born in Newport, New Hampshire, in July 1827, became an extremely successful lawyer and bank president by the time he reached the age of thirty-six years. In 1873, while on vacation from his New York banking company, he discovered the beautiful undeveloped beaches on Long Island. He promptly bought twenty-five miles of oceanfront, built a grand hotel and then built a railroad to transport wealthy New Yorkers to the beach. Although his earlier interests had made Corbin wealthy, his oceanfront development made him a multimillionaire.

Corbin retired at age fifty-nine and returned to Newport, where his most amazing undertaking was yet to come. He purchased some twenty-five

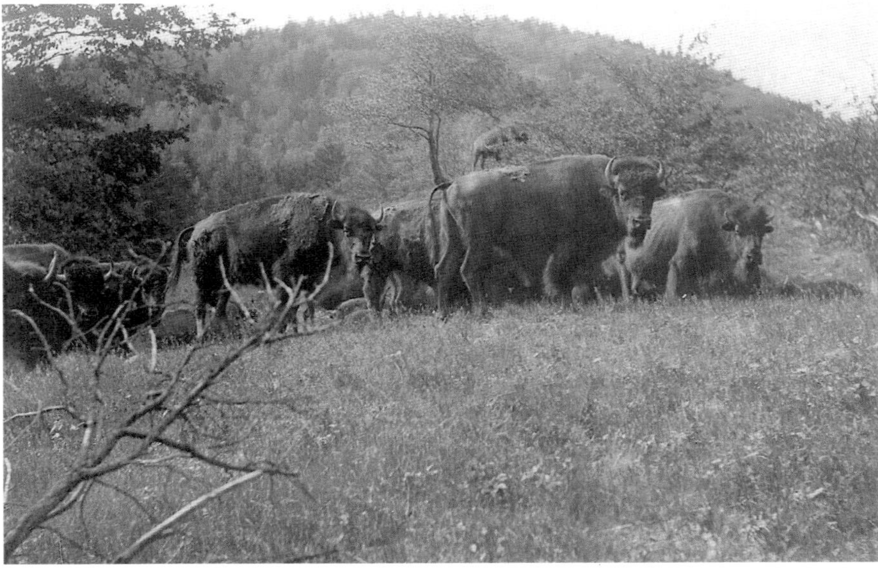

Buffalo at Corbin Park.

thousand acres in the towns of Newport, Croydon, Plainfield, Cornish and Grantham and built a thirty-mile fence around the property. He then began to stock the land with wild animals from across the country and around the world. He imported buffaloes, reindeer, moose, elk, several kinds of deer, antelopes, wild goats, wild boar from the Black Forest of Germany and many other creatures. Some animals were not successful in Corbin's park, but the deer, elk, boars and buffaloes thrived. It was largely through the effort of the park staff that the American bison was saved from extinction in this country. The Corbin family supported legislation to provide preserves for buffalo herds and often supplied the first animals for those preserves.

Austin Corbin was killed in a carriage accident near his Newport farm in 1896. His son continued to manage the park, which was open to the public for many years. No hunting was allowed until it became necessary to control the population of some of the animals. The park fell into disrepair after the death of Corbin's son, but it was revitalized in the 1940s as an exclusive membership organization. The new owners maintained Corbin's Park for game breeding and hunting purposes.

Visit us at
www.historypress.net

This title is also available as an e-book